ACPL, Laramie, WY   1/2019
3910200
Goldstor
Unpunis   re
Pieces:1

WITHDRA

D0599480

UNPUNISHED MURDER

MASSACRE AT COLFAX
AND THE
QUEST FOR JUSTICE

FOREWORD BY ANGELA ONWUACHI-WILLIG

UNPUNISHED MURDER

MASSACRE AT COLFAX AND THE QUEST FOR JUSTICE

LAWRENCE GOLDSTONE

SCHOLASTIC
FOCUS

NEW YORK

Albany County
Public Library
Laramie, Wyoming

A NOTE TO READERS:

This book includes quoted material from primary source documents, some of which contains racially offensive language. These passages are presented in their original, unedited form in order to accurately reflect history.

Copyright 2018 © by Lawrence Goldstone

All rights reserved. Published by Scholastic Focus, an imprint of Scholastic Inc., *Publishers since 1920.* SCHOLASTIC, SCHOLASTIC FOCUS, and associated logos are trademarks and/or registered trademarks of Scholastic Inc.

The publisher does not have any control over and does not assume any responsibility for author or third-party websites or their content.

No part of this publication may be reproduced, stored in a retrieval system, or transmitted in any form or by any means, electronic, mechanical, photocopying, recording, or otherwise, without written permission of the publisher. For information regarding permission, write to Scholastic Inc., Attention: Permissions Department, 557 Broadway, New York, NY 10012.

Library of Congress Cataloging-in-Publication Data available
ISBN 978-1-338-23945-4

10 9 8 7 6 5 4 3 2 1   18 19 20 21 22

Printed in the U.S.A. 23
First edition, September 2018

Book design by Keirsten Geise

TO NANCY AND LEE

TABLE OF CONTENTS

UNPUNISHED MURDER

MASSACRE AT COLFAX
AND THE
QUEST FOR JUSTICE

FOREWORD

AT THE END OF the prologue in *Unpunished Murder*, historian Lawrence Goldstone writes, "The story of Colfax, then, is the story of America." No truer words could be written. Yet very few Americans know the story of the Colfax Massacre, in which more than one hundred African-American men were slaughtered by white supremacists on Easter Sunday 1873.

For more than two centuries, our students have learned only partial truths about the racial hatred and denigration underlying much of our nation's history—for example, the false claim that slavery had nothing to do with the Civil War was widely taught for many years. It is important, perhaps now more than ever, to move past such myths, and to confront this nation's true racial history.

My own experiences as a student illustrate precisely why *Unpunished Murder* is such a vital contribution to young readers' literature. Too many of the history lessons I received during my primary and secondary school days in Texas public schools erased the impact that African-Americans, including slaves, made on the building and development of our nation, and sanitized the abominations of slavery and other racist systems and practices. As a young black student in the South, I not only felt alienated by the incomplete and, in some instances, inaccurate history that I was learning in the class-room, I also felt cheated by the fact that, in order to learn about African-American history, Mexican-American history, and Native American history, I had to seek out such knowl-edge for myself. I wish books like *Unpunished Murder* had been available to me then.

In this fine work, Lawrence Goldstone not only traces the complex and often inspiring experiment in self-government that was the United States, he also compellingly describes how its political system, and especially the United States Supreme Court, repeatedly failed to protect the rights of African-Americans. In fact, Goldstone details how, during and after Reconstruction, the Court went still further and actively opposed any effort to guarantee equal rights for black citizens. During this period, few Supreme Court decisions were more infamous than that which freed the Colfax Massacre defen-dants, a travesty that led directly to the horrors of Jim Crow.

Goldstone's retelling of the founding of Colfax, a town led by freedmen; the Colfax Massacre; two ensuing trials; and other events leading up to and following the tragic massacre is not only an honest and shrewd collection of many narratives of and about America, but it is also an American treasure in that he provides a solid foundation upon which readers can better understand the inequities and racial tensions that still exist in our society.

Unpunished Murder tells the story of a conflicted America that has long been ignored by many—a story about an

America that impressively charted a path toward becoming the most powerful country in the world, while never living up to its promise of genuine equality for African-Americans. It is a tale of unparalleled opportunity for whites through the Homestead Act, which provided many white settlers each with 160 acres of public land in the West, alongside the unfulfilled promise of 40 acres and a mule for each newly freed slave who had toiled on plantation soil.

In the end, after describing the events and lives that have undergirded the "great battles that determined not only the laws of a new nation, but also its soul," Goldstone proclaims that "[t]hose battles continue today." Indeed they do, but I for one am hopeful that, with the guidance of books such as *Unpunished Murder*, our souls—the nation's soul—will one day be healed.

Angela Onwuachi-Willig
Chancellor's Professor of Law
University of California, Berkeley School of Law

PROLOGUE

BLOODY EASTER—LEVI NELSON

IN 1873, EIGHT YEARS after the end of the Civil War, Levi Nelson was finally free to toil as a blacksmith for his own sake rather than for the white man who had owned him. He lived in Grant Parish, Louisiana, an isolated area on the Red River in the northcentral part of the state. There were many other "freedmen"—as emancipated slaves were called—in Grant Parish, more black residents than white.

Three years before, in 1870, the United States Constitution had been amended to guarantee adult African-American males the right to vote, a privilege unthinkable just a decade before. And so, for the first time in his life, Levi Nelson could choose to be governed by men whose skin color was the same as his own. In another radical change, Colfax, the parish seat, was home to a unit of the Louisiana militia commanded by William Ward, a black Union army veteran, and many of Ward's recruits were freedmen as well, although few of them had any military training.

If Levi Nelson's freedoms were new, so was the district in which he lived. Grant Parish had been created only in 1869, carved out of adjacent Winn and Rapides Parishes, both of which remained largely white. (A "parish" is the same as a "county.") Almost the entire area had been part of the Calhoun plantation, owned by Willie Calhoun, one of those rare Southern white men who believed that black people deserved the same rights as every other American. At Calhoun's urging, Louisiana's Republican legislature had created the new parish to give freedmen a base of political power. They had named it after President Ulysses S. Grant, and named the town after Vice President Schuyler Colfax. Republicans, the party of Abraham Lincoln and almost all African-Americans, had become a force in Southern politics since the United States Army had been sent into the conquered Confederacy to guarantee the very rights that Levi Nelson now enjoyed.

Democrats, virtually all of whom were white, loathed these changes—most considered freed slaves little more than beasts. The most ferocious of the white supremacists, who called themselves Redeemers, had banded together across the South in groups such as the Ku Klux Klan to fight any attempt to raise the political and economic status of freedmen. Their weapons were terror and murder. In one period, between April and November 1868, more than one thousand freedmen were murdered by whites.

In Grant Parish, the freedmen fought back. Colfax was the scene of a number of skirmishes, and in the first week of April

1873, whites attempting to take over the town government had been repeatedly beaten back by black defenders. On April 13, 1873, Easter Sunday, Redeemers decided once and for all to take Grant Parish back.

The invaders arrived at dawn—perhaps two hundred armed white men, some on horseback, others dragging a four-pound cannon. Many were Confederate war veterans and came armed with modern rifles, pistols, and shotguns. Some had journeyed from up to four hundred miles away to participate in the assault. Fearing this very sort of attack, William Ward had earlier ordered trenches to be dug around the courthouse. Ward himself had traveled to New Orleans to explain how desperate the situation was and to attempt to persuade the governor to send reinforcements.

Word had arrived days earlier of the impending Redeemer attack and many local black men, including Levi Nelson, along with women and children, perhaps four hundred in all, had gathered in and around the courthouse for protection. More than one hundred freedmen, about half of them armed, but only with antiquated shotguns, had taken up positions either in the courthouse or in the surrounding trenches.

One of the Redeemers' leaders, James W. Hadnot, a former Confederate colonel, was among the first to approach the town square. The cannon was brought into range. Although no one knows who fired first, shots were soon exchanged. The white men, who were deployed in a semicircle around the courthouse, were so eager that they fired wildly until another of their leaders, Christopher Columbus "C. C." Nash, also a former Confederate officer, screamed that they might be firing on their own men. Soon, three of the invaders, including Hadnot, were mortally wounded, Hadnot and one of the others likely shot by their own comrades. A number of the defenders had been shot dead as well.

The outcome of the battle was never in doubt. After six volleys from the cannon, the courthouse was set on fire, and the hopelessly outgunned freedmen gave up. The whites instructed the black men to stack their arms and march out, assuring them they would not be harmed.

The Redeemers moved through the ranks of their captives and collected their weapons. Then, as the prisoners were marched off, without warning, the white invaders opened fire.

Colfax was so difficult to get to that neither army units nor reporters could reach the town until days later. What they found shocked the nation. As the *New York Times* reported in a special dispatch, "It now appears that not a single colored man was killed until all of them had surrendered to the whites . . . when over 100 of the unfortunate negroes were brutally shot down in cold blood. It is understood that another lot of negroes was burned to death in the Court-house when it was set on fire." The killing had gone on well into the night and took place not only in the town, but also in the surrounding woods, where freedmen trying to flee were killed on sight. "The details of the massacre . . . are positively appalling in

Colfax victims.

their atrocity, and would appear to be more like the work of fiends than that of civilized men in a Christian country."

The Redeemers had been determined to kill every black man they could find, but some survived, many of them with terrible wounds. One survivor owed his life to a bit of hubris of one of the white invaders. The white man had bragged that he could kill two men with a single bullet fired at close range. The first man struck had died, but the bullet had lost sufficient velocity so that the second man was only wounded. That man lay on the ground until hours after dark, pretending to be dead, and then, after most of the Redeemers had left Colfax, he crawled into the woods.

And thus Levi Nelson lived to bear witness to what would be known in the North as the Colfax Massacre.

But not in the South. There, and in some Democratic newspapers in the North, such as the *Brooklyn Daily Eagle*, the incident was referred to as the Colfax Riot. The *Daily Eagle*, which boasted "the largest circulation of any evening newspaper published in the United States," blamed the incident entirely on the freedmen, claiming, without any proof or eyewitness testimony, that James Hadnot had been shot down in cold blood after offering a flag of truce, and that the white invaders had merely taken possession of government buildings that were rightfully theirs, all with a minimum of force. A memorial headstone was later erected in Louisiana in honor of the three Redeemers "who fell in the Colfax Riot fighting for white supremacy."

The tragedy of Colfax did not end with the massacre, however, but in the most hallowed courtroom in the land, a place where the Founding Fathers, in particular Alexander Hamilton, had promised that the rights of oppressed citizens would be protected.

The story of Colfax, then, is the story of America, and it begins where America began, in the State House in Philadelphia, now known as Independence Hall. From there, a new Constitution was issued, signed on September 17, 1787, which spawned a series of great battles that determined not only the laws of the new nation, but also its soul. Those battles continue today.

1

A NEW GOVERNMENT— ALEXANDER HAMILTON AND "BRUTUS"

WHEN INDEPENDENCE WAS SECURED by the Treaty of Paris of 1783, the United States was not really united at all. Under America's governing document, the Articles of Confederation, which called itself a "compact of friendship," each state was allowed to operate as almost a separate country—with its own laws, its own militia, even its own money. Such a system could not serve the needs of the new nation, but it would be difficult to change. Most Americans identified more with the state they lived in than with the United States.

Alexander Hamilton.

James Madison.

But some, like James Madison of Virginia and Alexander Hamilton of New York, believed the new nation could not grow, and perhaps not even survive, unless it truly became one. In May 1787, they tricked twelve of the thirteen states into sending delegations to Philadelphia, supposedly to reform the Articles. Rhode Island, nicknamed "Rogue's Island" for its freewheeling style in business, was perfectly happy with the Articles as they were and refused to send anyone to fix them. Once in this "convention," Madison and Hamilton intended to draft an entirely new system of laws and then to persuade the other delegates to accept it. But the odds were not good. The issues that divided the states were stronger than those that bound them together, and no issue divided the states more than slavery. Madison himself said, "The real difference of interests, lay not between large and small, but between the Northern and Southern states. The institution of slavery and its consequences formed a line of discrimination."

The delegates fought for four months behind locked doors, often in sweltering heat, and when the Convention finally ended, Hamilton, Madison, and their supporters had won. On September 17, 1787, in a ceremony both solemn and joyous, thirty-nine delegates, including the Convention's presiding officer, George Washington, signed the newly drafted Constitution of the United States.

The "Supreme Law of the Land" contained seven major divisions, called "Articles," the first three of which discussed who would govern and what powers those who were elected and appointed would have. Article I dealt with the legislature—Congress—which almost every delegate believed would be the most powerful branch of government. Congress was divided into two chambers, a House of Representatives, which would be elected directly by all those who were allowed to vote, and a Senate, whose members—two per state—would be chosen by state legislatures. (After the Seventeenth Amendment in 1913, senators, too, would be elected by popular vote.) Article I is by far the longest since, with the British Parliament as a model, there was a greater understanding of what a legislature should and should not be able to do.

But the British Parliament never had to deal with whether or not slaves would be counted for representation, while in the United States this question was of equal or even greater importance than anything else the delegates had to decide. The white slaveholding South wanted slaves to be counted to determine how many seats a state would be granted in the House of Representatives; the North, which had almost no slaves, was opposed.

1 — Objections to the present confederation

I Entrust the great interests of the nation to hands
   incapable of managing them —

   ~~Treaties of all kind~~

   All matters in which foreigners are concerned —

   The care of the public peace : Debts

   Power of treaty without power of execution

   Common defence without power to raise troops
   have a fleet — raise money

   — Power to contract debts without the power
   to pay —

   — These great interests of the state must be
   well managed or the public prosperity
   must be the victim —
   Legislates upon communities
   Where the Legislatures are to act they
   will deliberate —

   No sanction —   { To ask money not ...
                      { & by ... unjust mea...
                        Legal

989

Alexander Hamilton's June 1787 notes for a speech proposing a plan of
government at the Federal Convention.

4

July 14. 1787.   611.

of their assent to other necessary measures. 3. They could obtrude measures on the majority, by virtue of the peculiar powers which would be vested in the Senate. 4. The evil, instead of being cured by time, would increase with every new state that should be admitted, as they must all be admitted on the principle of equality. 5. The perpetuity it would give to the preponderance of the Northern against the Southern scale, was a serious consideration. It seemed now to be pretty well understood, that the real difference of interests lay, not between the large and small, but between the Northern and Southern, States. The institution of slavery, and its consequences, formed the line of discrimination. There were five states on the Southern, eight on the Northern side of this line. Should a proportional representation take place, it was true, the Northern would still outnumber the other, but not in the same degree, at this time; and every day would tend towards an equilibrium.

Mr. Wilson would add a few words only. If

Madison's July 14 notes, when he acknowledges that slavery is what most divides the nation.

5

The issue put delegates from both sections in an odd position. White Southerners, who usually insisted slaves were property, had to in this case insist they were people. Northerners, who were equally firm that human beings could not be property, had to here insist they were. In the end, they compromised. For every five slaves, three would be counted for deciding representation. Since slaves could not vote, this of course meant that the vote of a white man from a slaveholding state was worth more than one from a free state. If the North had not given in on this question, however, Southern delegates would have walked out, and the effort to draft a Constitution would have failed. The "Three-Fifths Compromise" became the best known, but not the only, accommodation that the North made in Philadelphia to the slaveholding South.

The delegates next turned to Article II, the election and powers of the president. Drawing up this article was more difficult—it took more than 160 different votes—because, although they knew they didn't want a king or queen, the delegates had no model on which to base an alternative. Deciding whether or not to call the president "Your Excellency" aroused passionate debate, and there were even proposals that the presidency be a council of three. In the end, although the president would be the commander in chief of the army and navy—almost all the delegates assumed the first president would be General Washington—he (and someday she) was not expected to be nearly as powerful as presidents turned out to be.

There was great disagreement on how the president should be elected. Very few of the delegates favored a popular vote, which would mean that each eligible individual voter had the same influence on the outcome as every other voter. Most delegates wanted the states to have the strongest voice. After much debate, the idea of an electoral college was agreed to. Under this system, each state would choose electors equal in number to its combined number of senators (always two) and members of the House of Representatives. With slaves giving Southern states more representatives than they would have been entitled to with only whites counted, this meant that slave states also got a larger voice in selecting a president. Each state was free to choose electors any way they wished, by popular vote, by the state legislature, or by any other formula they decided on.

One area of agreement was that the president should nominate judges to any court that came under federal control, although the Senate would have to ratify—vote to agree to— any appointment. Article II was a bit shorter than Article I, but still extensive.

Article III discussed the federal court system. It was by far the shortest of the first three Articles, and with good reason— most Americans did not want a federal court system at all, and certainly not one that had any real power. There were two main reasons for their distrust. First, in a country that did not even have enough money to afford a modern army and navy, any money spent to pay judges or build courthouses was thought wasted. But far more important was the fear that citizens of one state would be forced to stand in judgment before citizens of another—in effect, foreigners. Opponents of national courts—and there were many—were certain a national court system would quickly claim powers that were supposed to be reserved to the states.

As a result, Article III was short and extremely vague. While there was mention of a "Supreme Court," Article III did not say exactly how many judges would be on it. Nor did the delegates lay out completely what powers it would have, nor how courts other than the Supreme Court would be organized—or whether they would even exist at all. It was left to Congress to decide these questions after the Constitution was in place.

To get the Constitution in place, however, nine of the thirteen states would have to ratify the plan, and in many states ratification was uncertain. Although with New Hampshire's ratification on June 21, 1788, nine states had agreed and the Constitution was officially adopted, two of the most important states of the original thirteen—Virginia and New York—had yet to agree. Many people believed the new Constitution would be rejected by both. Rejection by either would be difficult to overcome—rejection by both would be a disaster.

In Virginia, the most important supporter was James Madison, and the most vocal opponent, Patrick Henry. Henry, famed for proclaiming, "Give me liberty or give me death," was the most brilliant orator in the entire nation. He would often speak for two or three hours before audiences that were so spellbound they barely breathed. He told his fellow Virginians that a national court system was a threat to their way of life. "They'll take your niggers from you," he warned his fellow delegates in the state convention Virginia had called to debate ratification. But Madison, also a slaveholder, was brilliant as well, and eventually, in a very close contest, Virginia agreed to ratify the Constitution.

That left New York, where the opposition—although lacking a Patrick Henry—was even more intense. While, in Virginia, the battle between those who favored the Constitution—"Federalists"—and its opponents—"Anti-Federalists"—was fought largely in the ratifying convention, in New York it was also fought in newspapers. In New York City, which was an Anti-Federalist stronghold, an opponent of the Constitution who wrote under the name Brutus published a series of essays—similar to modern op-eds—in which he attacked the Constitution as a document that would surely lead to tyranny. Giving the central government so much power would trample on the rights of the people.

Brutus, whose identity remains unknown, was particularly harsh about the new national court system, claiming it would be a tool with which the rich and powerful could oppress the ordinary citizen. About a Supreme Court whose members would never need to face an election and would serve for life, Brutus wrote, "I question whether the world ever saw a court of justice invested with such immense powers, and yet placed in a situation so little responsible . . . There is no power above them to control any of their decisions. There is no authority that can remove them, and they cannot be controlled by the laws of the legislature. In short, they are independent of the people, of the legislature, and of every power under heaven. Men placed in this situation will generally soon feel themselves independent of heaven itself."

Brutus seemed to be swaying New York against the Constitution, so in response, Alexander Hamilton, James Madison, and John Jay—writing jointly under the name Publius—published their own series of eighty-five essays in a competing newspaper. These essays were later published together as *The Federalist*, now also referred to as *The Federalist Papers*.

It fell to Hamilton to defend the new court system, which he did in one of the most famous of all the essays, *Federalist 78*. Hamilton fiercely denied that the court system would ever aid either of the two other branches in imposing unfair laws on the American people. Quite the reverse. The courts, particularly the Supreme Court, would be the "people's branch" of government, protecting against any attempt by either Congress or the president to pass laws or take action that would oppress ordinary citizens. In addition, Hamilton assured New Yorkers who feared the court system would rob them of their basic rights that the judicial branch of the new government would be "the weakest of the three."

THE

FEDERALIST:

A COLLECTION OF

E S S A Y S,

WRITTEN IN FAVOUR OF THE

NEW CONSTITUTION,

AS AGREED UPON BY THE

FEDERAL CONVENTION,

SEPTEMBER 17, 1787.

━━◆━━

IN TWO VOLUMES.
VOL. I.

━━◆━━

NEW-YORK:
PRINTED AND SOLD BY JOHN TIEBOUT,
No. 358 PEARL-STREET.
1799.

Cover page of *The Federalist*. All eighty-five essays were published together in 1799 and have been in print ever since.

As Madison had in Virginia, Hamilton won the day in New York, and on July 26, 1788, the Constitution was ratified.

Although North Carolina did not ratify until the following year and Rhode Island not until 1790, Madison and Hamilton had won their battle, and the new Constitution had become, as it promises in Article VI, the "Supreme Law of the Land."

2

THE SUPREME COURT IS BORN—
JOHN MARSHALL

THE CONSTITUTION HAD TWO major gaps that needed to be filled immediately. During the debates in Philadelphia, the Convention delegates had decided not to include a "Bill of Rights," a document that would protect "the people" from the new national government. They felt that since each state would be responsible for protecting its citizens, no listing of rights of individual Americans would be needed. But in the ratifying conventions, Federalists discovered that distrust of centralized power—the new national government—was greater than they had thought. Ratification would not have been possible without the promise that amendments (additions) to the new Constitution would be drafted as soon as the new government met.

The other requirement was, of course, to expand Article III and define what the federal court system would look like. How many courts would there be, how would their powers be divided, how many justices would sit on the Supreme Court?— all of these questions had been ignored in Philadelphia.

And so, in the 1st Congress, which began in Federal Hall in New York City on March 4, 1789, the same day George Washington took the oath of office to be the nation's first president, the first orders of business were those issues. (Travel was slow in those days, so the real business of governing did not begin until April, when Congress finally had the minimum number present to conduct business, called a "quorum.")

In the Judiciary Act of 1789, Congress declared that the court system would have three layers. At the top would be the Supreme Court, although the number of judges—to be called "justices"—remained undefined. Directly under the Supreme Court would be "circuit courts," which would be responsible for a section of the nation, usually more than one state. To save money, Supreme Court justices would also serve as circuit court judges, "riding circuit" twice a year. In a nation with few good roads and few inns along the way that served decent food, this requirement promised to be extremely unpopular among the justices. In fact, so unpleasant was riding circuit that some men refused appointments to the Supreme Court to avoid the chore. The lowest level of the federal judiciary would be the district courts, which would take cases from sections within states, so that people in a district would not feel that they were going to trial before "foreigners."

The federal courts could hear *only* cases that came under federal law. State courts would continue to hear cases under state law. Since the Constitution was supreme, if state law said one thing and federal law another, federal law would prevail. Almost every case under federal law would begin in district court. If the parties that lost a case were unhappy with the result and thought the district court had ruled unfairly or had not applied the law properly, they could "appeal" to the circuit court. If the circuit court agreed with the district court's ruling, they would "affirm" the decision. If they disagreed, they would "overturn" it. The same rule applied to circuit court rulings, except the losing party would then appeal to the Supreme Court.

The first Supreme Court consisted of six justices, with John Jay, a contributor to *The Federalist*, as the first chief justice. He would not stay in the job very long. During the Court's first session, the justices had no cases to hear and adjourned—ended the session—after a few minutes of ceremony. As the months progressed, it seemed that Hamilton had been correct—the court system would not only be the weakest of the three, but also the least busy. The Supreme Court continued to have so little to do that Jay accepted an assignment to sail to England on a diplomatic mission while continuing to serve as chief justice. He assumed he would not be missed on the Court, and he was not. Jay resigned

John Jay takes the bench.

soon afterward. His most impressive achievement as chief justice was choosing what robe to wear.

John Rutledge of South Carolina, who had been one of the most unapologetic defenders of slavery at the Constitutional Convention, was appointed by President Washington as Jay's successor. He presided over the Court for a short time before he was officially confirmed, but after rumors spread—possibly true—that he had gone insane, his nomination was rejected by the Senate. Oliver Ellsworth of Connecticut, who had been an important delegate at the Constitutional Convention and who had written the Judiciary Act of 1789, was Washington's next choice. Ellsworth was confirmed, but faced a shortage of work similar to Jay's, and accepted an appointment to travel as a diplomat to France.

Like Jay, Ellsworth resigned—while still in Paris—and President John Adams's secretary of state, Virginia's John Marshall, became chief justice. With Marshall's confirmation, everything changed, including the justices' dress. Marshall adopted simple black robes, a tradition that has remained largely in place until the present day. But in his modest clothing, Marshall became the most important chief justice the nation has ever seen.

In 1803, in *Marbury v. Madison*, considered the most important case the Supreme Court ever decided, Chief Justice Marshall established the concept of "judicial review," which gave the Supreme Court the power to declare a law unconstitutional. Since the Constitution was the supreme law of the land,

John Marshall was not as modest as he appeared.

any law that was in conflict with the Constitution had to be struck down even though Congress had passed it and the president had signed it. And since the Supreme Court, at least according to Marshall, had the power to "say what the law is," it was he and his fellow justices who would decide which laws would be enforced and which overturned. Judicial review turned out to be, by far, the most powerful weapon the Supreme Court could ever wield, and after more than two centuries, John Marshall is still hailed by legal scholars as the "Man Who Made the Court Supreme." Still, after *Marbury v. Madison*, judicial review was not used again to declare a law unconstitutional for more than fifty years, but when it was, it resulted in one of the most infamous decisions in American history.

3

LESS THAN HUMAN— ROGER TANEY AND DRED SCOTT

JOHN MARSHALL SERVED AS chief justice until his death in 1835 at age seventy-nine. Few men in the entire history of the United States have had a greater impact on how America is governed.

To the day he died, Marshall never wavered in his belief in a strong national government—and especially a strong national court system. But the president at the time of Marshall's death was Andrew Jackson, whose view of government—and the courts—could not have been more different. Jackson distrusted centralized power and insisted that, in most cases, states could and should do pretty much as they pleased. (After one of Marshall's Supreme Court rulings, in which the chief justice ruled that the state of Georgia could not seize lands from the Cherokee even though gold had been found there, Jackson is reported to have said, "John Marshall has made his decision. Now let him enforce it." Marshall could not, and Georgia took the land.)

"States' rights," as Jackson's philosophy was known, would of course ensure the continuation of slavery, since the government in Washington would lack the power to require any state to end it. Jackson was a slave owner himself and believed whites to be a superior race, fully justified in keeping black people as property. He was committed to protecting slavery from abolitionists in the North who were trying hard to prohibit it.

Jackson's reputation had been made in battles against Native American tribes—he was nicknamed "Indian Killer," which, sadly, was intended as a compliment. But it was during the War of 1812 that he became a national hero, when he teamed up with the pirate Jean Lafitte to defeat the British at the Battle of New Orleans. In his first try for the presidency,

Andrew Jackson.

in 1824, Jackson lost to abolitionist John Quincy Adams, even though Jackson had amassed more popular and electoral votes. A third candidate, Henry Clay, had received enough votes to deny either man victory. Clay disliked Adams but hated Jackson. When Clay threw his support to Adams, Jackson's supporters accused Clay and Adams of stealing the election, which Clay and Adams, by conspiring to deny the presidency to the man with the most support, may well have done.

Furious at losing to a man he despised, and disgusted with his own Democratic-Republican Party for letting it happen, Jackson decided to start a new political party. They called themselves the "Democrats." Four years later, the Democratic Party had its first victory when Jackson defeated Adams to become the seventh president of the United States.

When President Jackson took office, slavery had hardened the divisions between North and South to the point where the United States could easily have been thought of as two separate nations. Southerners were aware of how unpopular slavery was, not only in the North but in Europe as well, but were desperate to maintain the practice, which they were convinced was absolutely necessary to their way of life. Even more, the thought of slaves being freed and living among them as equals was both terrifying and disgusting to many.

But slavery was not simply a moral question—whether the enslavement of other human beings could be justified in a nation that called itself "the land of the free"—but was also an important political one. With three slaves out of every five counted to determine how many members a state would have in the House of Representatives—and in the Electoral College—slavery was the very foundation of Southern power in government. In fact, had slaves not been counted in the presidential race of 1800, John Adams would have defeated Thomas Jefferson and been reelected.

To take John Marshall's place as chief justice, then, President Jackson needed someone who could be counted on absolutely to support slavery and the interests of slave states, which meant that the new chief justice's personal and political beliefs would be as far from John Marshall's as possible.

And Jackson had just the man—Roger Brooke Taney of Maryland.

Like the president, Taney (pronounced taw-nee) was a slave owner whose family had been slave owners before him. He was born in 1777, one year after the signing of the Declaration of Independence; was educated by private tutors as a young boy, a common practice; and had gone on to Dickinson College in Carlisle, Pennsylvania, where he finished at the top of his class. While a student, he visited his home only twice, walking the entire distance to Baltimore, eighty-five miles, in less than three days.

Although not disadvantaged by the color of his skin, Taney had nevertheless experienced discrimination firsthand. His family was Roman Catholic, and in large sections of the country, Catholics had been forbidden by law from engaging in certain professions or even serving in government. In

Chief Justice Roger Brooke Taney.

Maryland, while Taney was growing up, Catholics had not been allowed to teach in local schools.

Taney had ongoing health problems. His eyesight was poor, which left him prone to headaches, and he was, by nature, a nervous man. "My system was put out of order by slight exposure," he wrote, "and I could not go through the excitement and mental exertion of a court, which lasted two or three weeks, without feeling, at the end of it, that my strength was impaired and I needed repose." But ill health did not stop him. He forged a very successful career as a lawyer, and then moved on to politics. At age twenty-nine, he married the sister of his friend, Francis Scott Key, who wrote America's national anthem, "The Star-Spangled Banner." With her, he would have seven children.

That Taney supported slavery in Maryland is without doubt. But in defending a Methodist minister who had been arrested for disturbing the peace for giving an antislavery speech to a large, mixed-race crowd, Taney made an odd pronouncement.

A hard necessity, indeed, compels us to endure the evil of slavery for a time; it was imposed upon us by another nation [Great Britain] while we were yet in a state of colonial vassalage. It cannot be easily or suddenly removed, yet, while it continues, it is a blot on our national character. Every real lover of freedom confidently hopes that it will effectually, though it must be gradually, be wiped away, and earnestly looks for the means by which this necessary object may be best attained.

Whether he believed what he said or not, the minister was acquitted—found not guilty.

When Andrew Jackson ran for president in 1824, Roger Taney became an enthusiastic supporter, agreeing with Jackson's commitment to states' rights. Although Jackson lost, he was grateful to Taney and decided he was a man to watch. In 1827, Taney became Maryland's attorney general, and the following year he ran Jackson's successful campaign in Maryland. In 1831, Jackson appointed Taney as attorney general of the United States, the highest law enforcement position in the nation. The following year, Taney proved to Jackson that he had chosen the right man to support his views.

In 1822, South Carolina had passed a law that said "seamen of African descent on board a ship entering a South Carolina port" could be arrested and jailed until the ship sailed again. The ship's captain would have to pay South Carolina for the cost of a sailor's imprisonment. If he didn't, he could be fined, and the sailor sold into slavery. This meant that free black men who were citizens of other countries could in effect be kidnapped on the streets of South Carolina and either held for ransom or sold into slavery. Foreign nations protested the law, and an American court had even ruled it unconstitutional, but South Carolina had ignored the ruling and continued to enforce it. As attorney general, Taney wrote an opinion supporting South Carolina, which, he said, had every right to enslave foreign sailors trespassing on its soil.

Three years later, after John Marshall died, Andrew Jackson nominated Roger Brooke Taney to be chief justice of the Supreme Court. Although his nomination was opposed by many Northerners, Taney was confirmed. He would serve for twenty-eight years. In 1857, when he was eighty years old, Taney was handed what would be his most important case, a question of slavery and freedom, the decision on which, he knew, might either end the debate over slavery or help send the United States hurtling toward civil war.

*   *   *

Dred Scott was born into slavery, likely in Southampton, Virginia, perhaps in 1799. Since detailed records were rarely kept for slaves, the exact place and date of his birth can only be guessed at. He was originally called Sam and was owned by a planter named Peter Blow. Young Sam likely lived in slave quarters, which were cold in winter, stifling in summer, and provided for little more than merely to keep slaves alive. That Blow was never successful in business would have made the slave accommodations that much more uncomfortable. Still, it does not appear that Sam was physically abused, and he was even allowed to be a playmate to Blow's sons, with whom he became friends.

In 1818, Blow moved his family and his slaves to Alabama in the hopes that he would have better luck growing cotton. He remained there for twelve years, until, in 1830, he gave up farming and bought a boardinghouse in St. Louis, Missouri. Two years later, Peter Blow, beset as always by financial problems, died.

Shortly before his death, however, to raise some money, he had sold Scott, who now went by the name Dred, to John Emerson, an army surgeon stationed in St. Louis. Scott, who had never learned to read or write, nonetheless became Emerson's personal servant. By all accounts, Dred Scott was a quiet, polite man who performed his duties well, and grew to be valued and trusted by Dr. Emerson.

In 1832, Missouri was a slave state as a result of an agreement drafted by Congress in 1820 known as the Missouri

Compromise. In that year, the United States consisted of twenty-two states, eleven slave and eleven free. But if Missouri, which had petitioned to join the Union as a slave state, were admitted, the balance would be broken. Although everyone wanted to see the nation expand, Northerners refused to be outnumbered. So a compromise was reached—Missouri was admitted as a slave state, but Maine also joined the Union as a free state. In addition, a boundary line running east to west was established above which no state—except Missouri—could allow slavery. Below the line, slavery would be permitted. Neither side liked the deal—Southerners were upset that Congress had been allowed to legislate slavery, and Northerners were forced to allow the official sanctioning of slavery below the compromise line. But both sides accepted it. Henry Clay, who was largely responsible for getting everyone to agree, became known as the "Great Pacificator."

As long as Dr. Emerson remained in St. Louis, then, there could be no argument about Dred Scott's status as a slave. But in 1833, Emerson was reassigned to Fort Armstrong, in Rock Island, Illinois, a free state, then three years later to Fort Snelling, in the Wisconsin territory, where slavery was prohibited by the Missouri Compromise. At Fort Snelling, Scott met Harriet Robinson, a slave owned by a local justice of the peace who married the two in either 1836 or 1837. Although slavery was prohibited in Wisconsin, the status of slaves brought into free states or territories from slave states, as Dred Scott and Harriet Robinson had been, was unclear. Most people assumed they remained slaves, as had been the custom since the Constitution had been adopted, but neither Congress nor the courts had issued a final say.

Marriage between slaves was rare because it was considered unnecessary by their white masters—slaves, after all, were not considered people—and this ceremony might have been the first time Dred Scott began to think he could be a free man. It certainly indicated the respect John Emerson must have felt for a man who had been his constant companion. Harriet gave birth to four children in free territory, two boys and two girls. The boys died soon afterward, but under the law, neither of the Scott daughters, Eliza and Lizzie, could be considered a slave.

For the next few years, both Emerson and the Scotts moved about, but in 1843, John Emerson died. Scott and his wife became the property of Emerson's wife, Irene Sanford Emerson, who returned them to her home in St. Louis. Irene's father was proslavery, and having little work himself for the Scotts, he hired them out to work for other families. Hiring out slaves was a common practice and John Emerson had on occasion done so himself.

On April 6, 1846, Dred and Harriet Scott sued for their freedom. Since they had lived in a territory where slavery was prohibited, and had even been married there, they claimed they had automatically become free. And once they were free, they could no longer ever be considered someone's property. The stakes of their lawsuit could not have been greater—if they won, every slave who set foot in a free state, even for one minute, became forever free.

Why they chose that particular time and how they gained the funds to get the necessary legal papers drawn up were never made totally clear. Although Missouri courts had usually ruled "once free, always free" when slaves sued for freedom, filing suit when they lived in a free state would have given the Scotts a much better chance of winning. But in any case, their lawsuit set in motion a series of events that would shake the nation.

It would, however, take ten years. As a result of a number of legal questions, a major fire and cholera epidemic in St. Louis, the transferring of ownership from Irene Emerson to her brother, John Sanford, and Sanford's move to New York, *Dred Scott v. Sandford* (the court clerk misspelled Sanford's name) did not reach the Supreme Court and Roger Taney until February 1856. Then, due to "differences of opinion" among the justices, the case was reheard in December 1856.

As the weeks and months dragged on, the legal issues became almost beside the point. Americans in both the North and South grew more and more on edge waiting for the Court to decide, as they saw it, nothing less than whether African-Americans were human beings under the law, and from there, whether slavery would survive or die.

Both Chief Justice Taney and the new president, James Buchanan, could not help but be aware of the enormous importance of the case. The nation seemed to need only a tiny shove

FRANK LESLIE'S
ILLUSTRATED

NEWSPAPER

No. 81.—VOL. IV.] NEW YORK, SATURDAY, JUNE 27, 1857. [PRICE 6 CENTS.

Dred Scott and his wife, Harriet, and their two daughters.

to descend into civil war. Both seemed to believe that only a firm statement, leaving no doubt of the Court's position, would settle the question and allow the nation to move forward.

And a firm statement was what the chief justice produced. But if he or President Buchanan thought it would serve to end the debate over slavery, they could not have been more wrong.

The decision was 7–2, with the five slave-owning justices joined by two others who had been badgered by Taney and likely Buchanan to keep the decision from breaking purely on North-South lines. Taney wrote the majority opinion himself. In it, he said, African-Americans "had for more than a century before been regarded as beings of an inferior order, and altogether unfit to associate with the white race, either in social or political relations; and so far inferior, that they had no rights which the white man was bound to respect; and that the negro might justly and lawfully be reduced to slavery for his benefit."

As a matter of law, then, Dred Scott remained a slave, and his tenure in free states could not affect that status. What is more, since no person descended from an American slave had ever been a citizen of the United States as defined in the Constitution, they could not be citizens of a state either. By this definition, the Scotts' children would be slaves along with their parents. Only Congress could grant national citizenship, and they had not done so for slaves. Finally, since slaves were only property, and no man or state could seize the property of someone else without "due process of law," the Missouri Compromise was unconstitutional.

Reaction was predictable. The decision was denounced in the North and praised in the South. The *Chicago Daily Tribune* wrote that the decision would be "regarded, throughout the Free States and wherever the pulse of Liberty beats, only as the votes of five slaveholders and two doughfaces [Northerners with Southern sympathies] upon a question where their opinion was not asked, and where their votes would not count." But the South Carolina's *Charleston Mercury* wrote that "the sanction of the deliberate judgment of the highest tribunal in the land" supported slave states' "claim to equality of privilege."

But it was Frederick Douglass who got to the heart of the matter in a speech to the American Anti-Slavery Society in New York on May 14, 1857. "It is clearly not because of the peculiar character of the Constitution that we have slavery, but the wicked pride, love of power, and selfish perverseness of the American people. Slavery lives in this country not because of any paper Constitution, but in the moral blindness of the American people, who persuade themselves that they are safe, though the rights of others may be struck down."

Seven years later, in October 1864, in the midst of the horrible war he had failed to prevent, Roger Brooke Taney died. Although many spoke highly of Taney's personal qualities, and his record was defended by friends, the author of the *Dred Scott* decision was condemned after his death to a degree never before seen in American history. Newspapers, members of Congress, and even other judges described the departed chief justice as a blight on American democracy. One editorial, in Philadelphia's *North American*, said, "History will expose him to eternal scorn in the pillory she has set up for infamous judges." The *New York Times*, while praising Taney as "a man of pure moral character and great legal learning," observed that the *Dred Scott* decision was "an act of supreme folly, and its shadow will ever rest upon his memory." A move to erect a bust of Taney next to that of his predecessor, John Marshall, was blocked by outraged congressmen.

Dred Scott finally obtained his freedom. Peter Blow's sons, his childhood friends, had supported his suit and helped pay his legal expenses. In May 1857, they bought Dred and Harriet Scott and immediately granted them their freedom.

But Scott did not enjoy being a free man for long. Still unable to read or write, he was hired as a porter by a hotel in St. Louis. A little more than one year later, Dred Scott died of tuberculosis. Harriet Scott lived two decades as a free woman before her death in 1876.

Lizzie Scott lived to be ninety-nine years old but never had children. Eliza Scott married and had at least one child. On March 6, 2017, on the steps of the Maryland State House, next to the statue of Roger Taney, placed there in his honor, Taney's great-great-grandnephew, Charles Taney III, publicly apologized for the great injustice of the *Dred Scott* decision to Lynne Jackson, the Scotts' great-great-granddaughter.

Five months later, on August 6, 2017, that statue was removed.

4

REMAKING AMERICA—
ANDREW JOHNSON AND
THADDEUS STEVENS

BEFORE THE ELECTION OF Abraham Lincoln in 1860, the American government was tiny. In a nation of thirty-four million people spread across almost two million square miles, only nine thousand men—and some women—worked for the federal government. (Another twenty-five thousand were in the army or the navy.) Most Americans grew up in the countryside and, except for trips to nearby towns, did not travel a great deal, so many might have gone their entire lives and never met a federal government employee.

After the Civil War ended in 1865, however, all that had changed. Millions had fought in the war and hundreds of thousands remained on Union army and navy payrolls. In addition, the ranks of nonmilitary employees had swelled to 53,000. The federal government had grown from being nearly invisible to becoming the largest employer in the United States.

In a nation just recovering from a bloody and costly war, putting all those people out of work was not a possibility. Nor, as it turned out, was it necessary. Reuniting America would require the federal government to provide services that could not have been imagined four years earlier. The hundreds of thousands of war wounded needed to be cared for, pensions for soldiers and their families had to be administered, shelter needed to be provided for the homeless, and the economy of the South, where much of the land had been laid waste, had to be restored. But by far the most immense, most difficult, and most daunting task was to find a way to integrate four million newly freed slaves into the mainstream of American life. No nation in history had ever faced such a challenge. That this undertaking would unfold in a section of the nation in which African-Americans were loathed and thought to be an inferior species of human being would make the job that much harder.

The effort began in March 1865, even before the war ended, when Congress voted to establish a Bureau of Refugees, Freedmen, and Abandoned Lands to distribute food and clothing, and establish schools and medical facilities for freedmen. Three weeks later, Robert E. Lee surrendered to Ulysses S. Grant at Appomattox Court House, and every slave in the defeated Confederacy was legally free. The Freedmen's Bureau was cheered in the North as a solid first step but detested in the South, especially after white Southerners learned that the agency would be part of the War Department and be headed by an army general, Oliver O. Howard. (Howard went on to use federal funds to begin a college in Washington, DC, Howard University, where freedmen and people of all races and creeds could study, and which remains a highly ranked college with an international reputation.) To white people of the South, this was occupation by foreigners—not, as President Lincoln had promised in his second inaugural address, an honest attempt "to bind up the nation's wounds." Even more infuriating for white Southerners was the announcement that military courts, rather than their own court system, would deal with offenses against black Americans.

In order to show that he was president of *all* the people, Lincoln, a Republican, had chosen Andrew Johnson, a Democrat from Tennessee, to be vice president for his second term. Johnson and Lincoln disagreed on some important issues, but Lincoln did not intend his vice president to be much more than a gesture to his opponents. But only five days after Lee surrendered, Abraham Lincoln was dead, assassinated by John Wilkes Booth at Ford's Theatre in Washington, DC, and the gesture became the seventeenth president of the United States.

Becoming president would have been a dream without any chance of fulfillment when Andrew Johnson was a boy. He was born in Raleigh, North Carolina, on December 29, 1808, like Abraham Lincoln, in a log cabin. His father scratched out a living farming and doing odd jobs, and his mother took in laundry. The family became that much poorer when Johnson's father died trying to save a friend from drowning when Andrew was four years old. At ten, with no schooling and unable to read or write, Andrew became a tailor's apprentice. With the help of a coworker, Johnson taught himself to read.

Freedmen's school, South Carolina.

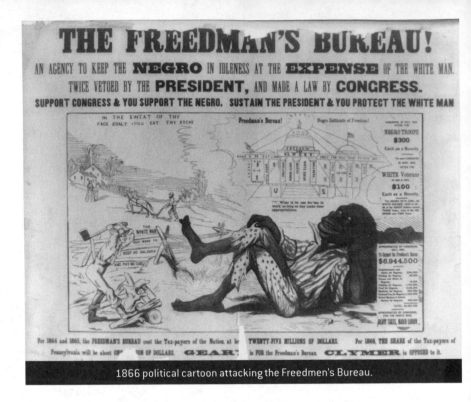

1866 political cartoon attacking the Freedmen's Bureau.

When he was sixteen, he and his brother ran away from the tailor shop, where he had been legally bound to work until he was twenty-one. They traveled to South Carolina, where Andrew supported himself tailoring, and two years after that, he moved to Tennessee.

Johnson eventually settled in Greeneville, and there fortune smiled on him. While running his business in the front of his home, he met Eliza McCardle, the daughter of a local shoemaker. They were married when Johnson was eighteen and his bride only sixteen. They would remain married for fifty years. Eliza was educated and refined, and taught Johnson

Andrew Johnson.

to write and basic mathematics, and helped him satisfy a thirst for learning that grew with each passing year.

By his young twenties, Andrew Johnson was already making a success of himself in local politics, serving as first alderman and then as Greeneville's mayor. In 1834, still only twenty-six, he helped frame a new state constitution, and was then elected to the Tennessee state legislature. In 1843, he won a seat in Congress, and ten years later was chosen as Tennessee's governor. In 1857, he was elected to the United States Senate for a six-year term. In each of these jobs, he was admired by both his coworkers and ordinary Tennesseans for hard work, honesty, and a commitment to helping working people. He had also developed a deep dislike for the rich—large landowners, bankers, and anyone who made their fortune from the toil of others.

In the Senate, Andrew Johnson continued his support for the ordinary American. He supported the Homestead Act, a unique opportunity for small farmers. Homesteaders who wished would be granted 160 acres of public land in the West, and if they lived and worked there for five years, the property would become theirs. Johnson later explained why he favored the policy: "The lands in the hands of industrious settlers, whose labor creates wealth and contributes to the public resources, are worth more to the United States than if they had been reserved as a solitude for future purchasers." The Homestead Act eventually resulted in the settling of eighty million acres of public land.

What had most brought Johnson to the attention of President Lincoln, though, was his fierce opposition to secession and, rare for a Tennessean, a dislike of slavery. When Tennessee seceded in 1861, Andrew Johnson retained his loyalty to the United States, the only congressman in the entire Confederacy to do so. When Union troops retook Tennessee in 1862, Lincoln appointed Johnson military governor, where he was firm and fair in administering his now conquered home state. Two years later, for his second term, Lincoln chose thrifty, serious, honorable Andrew Johnson to be his vice president.

In those first weeks after Lincoln's tragic assassination, it appeared that the martyred president had chosen well. Johnson promised to carry out Lincoln's plans and left all of Lincoln's cabinet officers in place. Andrew Johnson seemed to have the opportunity to become one of America's greatest presidents, the former tailor who sewed the divided nation back together.

But if all of his previous jobs had brought out the best in Andrew Johnson's character, his new job brought out the worst. Congressional leaders found the new president to be moody, stubborn, suspicious of the motives of others, and reacting to disagreements as if they were personal insults. He was determined to handle Reconstruction in his own way, and his idea of how to do it came from two firmly held beliefs.

First, like his fellow Tennessean Andrew Jackson, Johnson distrusted the central government and wanted states to retain

Lincoln, the rail-splitter, and Johnson, the tailor, repairing the nation.

the power to do pretty much as they pleased. As a result, he made no attempt to ensure that the post–Civil War governments of the Confederate states were any different from the white supremacist governments that had been in place before and during the war.

And so, although the Thirteenth Amendment to the Constitution stated, "Neither slavery nor involuntary servitude . . . shall exist within the United States," when these new governments passed laws that treated black Americans as if they were still slaves, Johnson was perfectly content to let them do so. These laws—Black Codes, as they came to be known—were openly racist and denied newly freed slaves the freedoms they thought they had been granted. In Louisiana, for example, the state legislature resolved, "We hold this to be a Government of White People, made and to be perpetuated for the exclusive benefit of the White race, and . . . that the people of African descent cannot be considered as citizens of the United States."

Black Codes contained provisions that, for example, forced black people to work for whites for long periods of time for almost no money, prohibited African-Americans from carrying knives or guns, set sunup to sundown working hours, allowed employers to beat their workers, and prevented freed slaves from traveling where they pleased. Under Black Codes, strict racial segregation was also required in schools, public buildings, and cemeteries.

Second, it also turned out that Johnson's opposition to slavery was not because it was morally wrong but because it strengthened the large landowners he so disliked, and helped create what he called a "slaveocracy." In fact, Johnson was consumed by a deep and abiding racism and was determined that freed slaves never be part of the political process. In a message to Congress shortly after taking office, he said:

> **If anything can be proved by known facts, if all reasoning upon evidence is not abandoned, it must be acknowledged that in the progress of nations, negroes have shown less capacity for government than any other race of people. No independent government of any form has ever been successful in their hands. On the contrary, wherever they have been left to their own devices they have shown a constant tendency to relapse into barbarism.**

But in his willingness to allow the defeated Confederacy to reinstitute slavery in everything but name, Andrew Johnson would come up against a group whose commitment to equal rights was as fervent as any in American history. To these congressmen, nothing was more important, more necessary for America's national honor, than for the four million freedmen to be allowed to participate as equals in every facet of American life. They demanded without compromise that African-Americans in the conquered South be granted full and equal citizenship with whites; they must be allowed to own businesses, enter into contracts, walk, ride, or live freely anywhere in the United States, and have equal access to schools, hospitals, and even cemeteries.

They were called Radical Republicans and were led in the House of Representatives by Thaddeus Stevens of Pennsylvania.

Stevens and Johnson had come from remarkably similar beginnings. Like Johnson, Stevens was born into poverty, in Danville, Vermont, in 1792. Also like Johnson, Stevens was raised by a single mother, although in his case, his father did not die but abandoned the family. Each would pull himself out of poverty through hard work and commitment, and as a result, each developed a dislike for large landowners and moneyed interests. Stevens would later say of plantation owners, "Strip a proud nobility of their bloated estates, reduce them to a level with plain republicans, send them forth to labor, and teach their children to enter the workshops or handle the plow, and you will thus humble proud traitors."

But the two men's attitudes toward African-Americans and equal rights could not have been more different. Where Andrew Johnson would announce, "Before I would see this Government destroyed I would send every negro back to Africa, disintegrated and blotted out of space," Stevens would insist, "No government can be free that does not allow all its citizens to participate in the formation and execution of her laws."

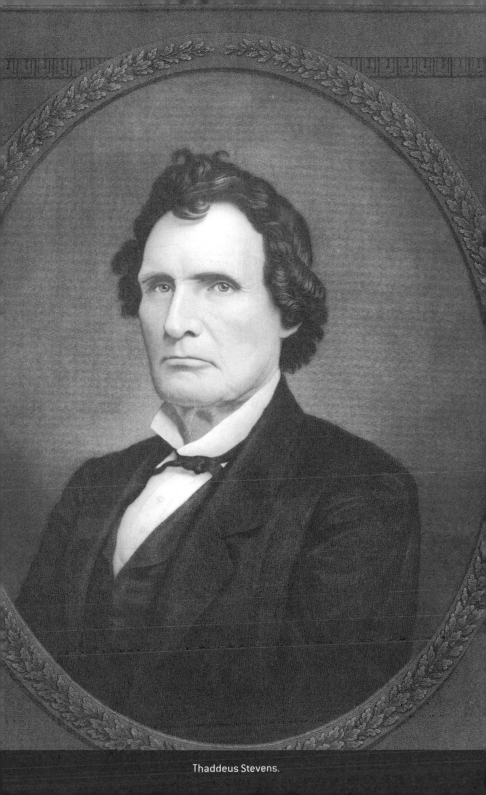

Thaddeus Stevens.

Stevens had moved to York, Pennsylvania, after graduating from Dartmouth College and, while studying law at night, taught in a one-room schoolhouse during the day. He came by his fervent belief in the rights of all Americans as a lawyer in Gettysburg, the site of the great Civil War battle to come, but in the 1840s a town on the Maryland border that was a frequent crossing point for runaway slaves. Stevens thought it un-Christian and inhuman that these terrified, cold, and hungry men, women, and children were forced to flee for their freedom—and often their lives—with only the clothes on their backs. When runaways were sued by their former masters, which happened frequently, Stevens would defend them without a fee.

As had Andrew Johnson, Thaddeus Stevens began in local politics, then moved on to state government. There he spoke out against slavery, Andrew Jackson and his Democratic Party, and promoted education and improvements in public services. Where Johnson saw national government as the enemy of freedom, Stevens viewed the legislature as the best place for securing it. During this time, he also became active in the Underground Railroad, which helped runaway slaves find sanctuary either in remote areas of the United States or in Canada.

In 1849, Thaddeus Stevens was elected to the United States House of Representatives, and in 1856, he joined the newly formed Republican Party. Throughout the Civil War, he urged his colleagues to enact antislavery legislation, and kept pressure on President Lincoln to emancipate the slaves. But even when Lincoln issued the Emancipation Proclamation on January 1, 1863, Stevens was upset because it did not free slaves in areas controlled by the United States government. (The Proclamation only freed slaves in areas controlled by the Confederacy, not in states such as Maryland, which had remained in the Union. As such, any slave who escaped to Union territory would be declared free, but slaves already in the Union would remain in bondage.)

In December 1863, Stevens helped draft the Thirteenth Amendment, which would abolish slavery throughout the United States. The amendment faced strong opposition from the Democratic Party, and it failed to gain the two-thirds necessary in the House. (An amendment, according to Article V of the Constitution, must be passed with two-thirds of the vote in both houses of Congress, and then be ratified by three-quarters of the state legislatures.) But with President Lincoln doing all he could to persuade or threaten reluctant congressmen, and after Stevens delivered the closing remarks in a debate on January 13, 1865, the amendment eventually garnered the two-thirds vote it needed. "The greatest measure of the nineteenth century was passed by corruption, aided and abetted by the purest man in America," Stevens said afterward.

After Lincoln's assassination, Stevens and his fellow Radical Republicans were relieved when President Johnson announced that he intended to continue to implement Lincoln's plan for remaking the South, which was called Reconstruction. Soon, however, it became clear that Andrew

Johnson intended to do no such thing. When white supremacist state governments passed Black Codes throughout the conquered South with Johnson's support, Stevens attacked. The United States would care for the freed slaves, and he left no doubt as to why it should and would be so:

> **We have turned or are about to turn loose four million slaves without a hut to shelter them or a cent in their pockets. The infernal laws of slavery have prevented them from acquiring an education, understanding the commonest laws of contract, or managing the ordinary business of life. This Congress is bound to provide for them until they can take care of themselves. If we do not furnish them with homesteads, and hedge them around with protective laws; if we leave them to the legislation of their late masters, we had better have left them in bondage.**

A commitment to feed, clothe, educate, and house millions of freedmen was going to cost a lot of money, so the Radical Republicans proposed paying for it by selling off the property of leaders of the Confederacy. In the end, each adult freedman would be given "40 acres and a mule" to start his own farm.

The Radical Republicans intended no less than to forcibly abolish racial inequality and all traces of racial discrimination, including changing Southern whites' belief that

African-Americans were inferior and undeserving of equality. Stevens said of his program, "It is intended to revolutionize their feelings and principles. This may startle feeble minds and shake weak nerves. So do all great improvements."

But black Americans had not emerged from slavery into a nation eager to embrace their new status as free men and women. To most whites, they were simply a burden on society. "Slavery is dead," the *Cincinnati Enquirer* announced at the end of the war, "the negro is not. There is the misfortune."

That most Americans, from the North or South, did not agree with spending so much money on a group of people so despised did not bother the Radicals at all. To them, racial equality was a crusade, and, thanks to Andrew Johnson's venomous racism, they were determined to acquire enough power in Congress to make their crusade law.

The two men whose careers embodied the opportunity that seemed unique to the United States were about to clash. The ferocious battle that ensued would eventually destroy the dreams of both of them.

5

SOME ODD ARITHMETIC—
WHO WON THE WAR?

BUT ANDREW JOHNSON WAS not the only problem Thaddeus Stevens and his fellow Radicals faced in their crusade to ensure equal rights for all Americans. There were also two questions of law.

The first seemed simple—were the states of the old Confederacy still part of the Union or not? Everyone in the North, from President Lincoln on down, had insisted that secession—states leaving the Union—was illegal. If Lincoln was correct, were those Confederate states still part of the United States and, now that the war was over, did they have every right to send representatives to Congress? Andrew Johnson thought so. He insisted that the eleven former Confederate states, now that their "rebellion" had been put down, had every right to return to a nation that they had never actually left.

The second question sprang from the first. If those states *were* still in the Union (or even if they were not but were readmitted later), how many congressmen did they deserve in the

House of Representatives? In 1862, 57 of the 241 seats in the House of Representatives had been granted to the eleven states that had seceded the year before—but since secession was illegal, those assigned seats remained empty. Those numbers, however, had been arrived at using the old three-fifths rule. In December 1865, with the ratification of the Thirteenth Amendment, slavery was abolished. Did that mean freedmen would now be counted in full? The *Dred Scott* decision said that slaves could never be citizens, yet now there were no slaves. The one absolutely necessary building block to everything the Radicals wanted to achieve was that freedmen be granted full and equal citizenship. Freedmen, therefore, must be counted equally with whites.

As a result, if Andrew Johnson and his fellow Democrats were correct, the eleven slave states could simply retake their places in Congress *in a stronger position than when they had left*. The South would *increase* their seats in the House of Representatives and have a stronger voice in the Electoral College as a result of *losing* the Civil War. And if *this* were true, and only white people were allowed to vote, the losers of the war might quickly turn into the winners.

But voting was a very thorny issue as well. Voting was the one basic right that even most Radicals were not certain should be granted immediately. After all, they reasoned, most former slaves could not read or write, had no schooling or experience in citizenship, and had spent their lives existing in conditions that in no way resembled the society that freedom had made them a part of. As such, freedmen might be tricked into voting—by white Democrats, the Radicals feared—for a candidate they did not really want. Freedmen voting for their former masters was every bit as bad as their not voting at all. Perhaps worse. Many Radicals thought the right to vote should be granted only after freedmen had received enough education to cast their ballots wisely.

But as Radicals digested the arithmetic of the Thirteenth Amendment, none of this mattered. Freedmen must be granted the right to vote as soon as possible, and they must cast their votes for the party that wished to protect them—Republicans.

Another way to help ensure Republican state governments in the South would be to take away the vote from white Democrats. To the Radicals, anyone who had fought for or helped the rebels had lost the privileges of citizenship. Former Confederates, like the states in which they lived, could only rejoin the Union if they pledged allegiance to the United States and vowed to always follow its laws. What the Radicals did not say, but what was understood, was that to rejoin the Union, both individuals and states would need to accept the Radical program, including full equality for African-Americans.

The first showdown took place in December 1865, when, with President Johnson's encouragement, the eleven former slave states did indeed send representatives to Congress. Each one was white, a former Confederate, and determined to protect the Black Codes. One of these would-be congressmen was Alexander Stephens, who had been vice president of the Confederacy. While the white Southerners waited to take their seats, the men in charge of both the House of Representatives and the Senate simply refused to call their names during the roll call. Thaddeus Stevens told them that they were from "conquered provinces" and not entitled to sit in Congress. The Southern delegates left; Andrew Johnson was furious; and the war between the president and Congress had begun.

Stevens and his supporters launched a full assault. The first order was to ensure basic rights of citizenship for freedmen, so on January 5, 1866, Senator Lyman Trumbull of Illinois introduced "A Bill to Protect All Persons in the United States in Their Civil Rights and Liberties." The Civil Rights Act of 1866 was to be the first civil rights law ever enacted by the United States Congress.

The bill was aimed squarely at the Black Codes. It guaranteed fundamental rights to freedmen, starting with the most fundamental right of all—citizenship. "All persons born in the United States and not subject to any foreign power . . . are hereby declared to be citizens of the United States." The *Dred Scott* decision was to be buried once and for all. Freedmen were also guaranteed the right to enter into contracts (and therefore own homes and businesses), access to the legal system (so they could sue anyone who wronged them), the right to employment, and the "full and equal benefits of all laws and proceedings for the security of person and property." Denial of any of these rights became a federal crime, enforceable according to federal law, in federal and not state courts.

Absent, however, was the guarantee of the right to vote. Although the Radicals needed such a provision to keep Southern whites from gaining too much power in Congress, there was not enough support to get it passed, so they decided to attack that problem separately. Without the right to vote, freedmen would also be prevented from sitting on juries, since jurors were selected from current voting rolls.

Andrew Johnson fought back the only way he could. He vetoed the bill—rejected it. According to the Constitution, if a president rejects a bill, two-thirds of both houses must vote for it in order to make it law—a measure known as "overriding" a veto. The Republican-dominated Congress did just that, and on April 9, 1866, the United States had its first law that asserted the rights of African-Americans.

At the time, just after the war's end, most Americans—at least in the North, but also some in the South—thought the new law was fair. Slavery had been a national horror and a good number of whites, at least at the time, felt honor bound to provide some basic protections to freed slaves. Most Democrats, of course, particularly in the South, complained that the bill was a terrible violation of states' rights—Andrew Johnson agreed—and also a violation of the principles under which the United States had been founded and, most important, unconstitutional. In this last point, some Radicals secretly agreed. They feared that the Supreme Court sometime

Passage of the Civil Rights Act of 1866.

in the future, particularly if Democrats took power, might overturn the law.

To protect these freedoms, then, Republicans needed to put them in a place where Johnson, the Democrats, and even the Supreme Court could never get at them.

The Constitution.

6

TWO AMENDMENTS AND A DREAM OF EQUALITY— JOHN BINGHAM

THERE ARE TIMES WHEN great figures are lost to history. John Bingham, a congressman from Ohio, is one of those. It is to Bingham that we owe an amendment that attempted—and for a time succeeded—to purge the sins of slavery and racism from the American Constitution.

Bingham was born in Pennsylvania in 1815. His father, Hugh, a carpenter, was also an abolitionist who occasionally had dealings with the Speaker of the Pennsylvania General Assembly, Thaddeus Stevens. When John was twelve, his father's wife died, but Hugh soon remarried and headed west. John could not get along with his new stepmother and was sent to Ohio to live with his uncle.

His uncle was also an abolitionist and so, in 1835, John enrolled at Franklin College, which was led by a member of the Underground Railroad. There, Bingham became friends with Titus Basfield, a former slave who would become the first black person to receive a college degree in Ohio. The two remained in touch for forty years.

John Bingham.

In his twenties, Bingham was a lawyer in Ohio and active in politics. One of his main goals was to keep slavery from expanding in the western territories. He became close friends with Salmon P. Chase, who would become secretary of the treasury under President Lincoln and chief justice of the Supreme Court after the death of Roger Taney. In 1854, Bingham joined the Republican Party and was elected to Congress.

From the first, Bingham became recognized as an important antislavery force and one of the most persuasive speakers in the House. He proclaimed that the Constitution was "based upon the equality of the human race. Its primal object must be to protect each human being within its jurisdiction in the free and full enjoyment of his natural rights." He told his fellows that black men, too, had fought for the nation's freedom, endured "the terrible trial of battle," and therefore deserved freedom themselves.

Although Bingham hoped Salmon Chase would be the Republican presidential nominee in 1860, after the election he became very close to Abraham Lincoln. "He was the saddest man I ever met," Bingham would say later, but "few men could illustrate a point better than Lincoln by a homely story. There was always playful humor about him which seemed to be thoroughly incorporated in his nature, as a kind of offset against his constitutional sorrow and sadness."

For his struggles both to aid the war effort and to promote equal rights, Bingham was defeated for reelection in 1862 in a district that had lost its taste for the war and turned sharply Democratic. Lincoln then appointed him to act as a government lawyer, prosecuting those accused of aiding the Confederacy. Bingham won back his seat in 1864 and, after the president was gunned down by John Wilkes Booth, was one of the three prosecutors of Booth's associates and gave the closing argument at their trial. All were hanged.

Congress had created a Joint Committee on Reconstruction to supervise the readmission of the Southern states into the Union, and both Thaddeus Stevens and John Bingham were key members. When it came time to draft an amendment to the Constitution to ensure citizenship and equal treatment under the law for black Americans—which would be the Fourteenth Amendment—Bingham did much of the work.

In the end, he wrote one of the most important clauses in the entire Constitution, which is in the first section of the Fourteenth Amendment. "No state shall make or enforce any law which shall abridge the privileges or immunities of citizens of the United States; nor shall any state deprive any person of life, liberty, or property, without due process of law; nor deny to any person within its jurisdiction the equal protection of the laws." The original language in the committee's draft restricted the provision to matters of race, but Bingham wanted the guarantees applied to every American. He said later that the clause was "a simple, strong, plain declaration that equal laws and equal and exact justice shall hereafter be secured within every State of the Union." The law must guarantee equal protection for "any person, no matter whence he comes, or how poor, how weak, how simple—no matter how friendless."

This was as eloquent a definition of the promise of American democracy as has ever been given, and one of the most important passages ever written to promote equal rights. The first section of the Fourteenth Amendment would eventually become the basis for desegregating public schools, guaranteeing voting rights, and forbidding gender discrimination.

In addition, as far as Bingham and his fellow Republicans were concerned, with this amendment, the "privileges and immunities" guaranteed in the Bill of Rights, which until this point had only applied to *federal* law, would now also apply to the states. But a mere ten years later, the Supreme Court would demonstrate that no language was ironclad if not backed up by the goodwill of those interpreting it.

Also in the first section of the amendment was "All persons born or naturalized in the United States, and subject to the jurisdiction thereof, are citizens of the United States and of the State wherein they reside." (Which is why, to this day,

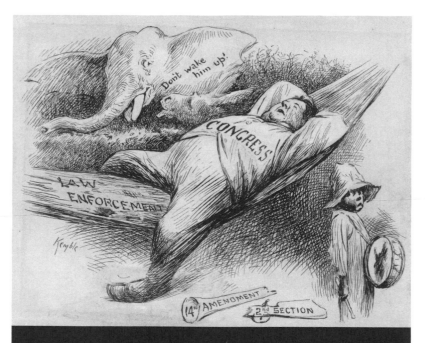

Republicans warn an African-American boy not to wake up a sleeping Congress, so that the part of the Fourteenth Amendment that will reduce white Democratic influence in the House of Representatives can go into effect.

children of immigrants born in the United States, whether those immigrants are in the country legally or not, automatically become citizens.) Freedmen, then, could not be denied any of the rights, the "privileges and immunities," that any white citizen enjoyed, by either federal or state government. While it did not address voting directly, few could doubt that the right to vote, at least for adult males, was a privilege of citizenship.

The second section of the amendment addressed the change from three-in-five to fully counting freedmen for seats in the House of Representatives. It said that if the right to vote was denied to any adult male, twenty-one or older, "except for participation in rebellion, or other crime," those voters would also be taken off the count for representation. While not guaranteeing freedmen the vote, it prevented Southern whites from gaining a bonus by *denying* them the vote.

The third section barred former Confederates from serving in state or national government unless amnesty was agreed to by two-thirds majority in both houses of Congress. The fourth section prevented Confederates from being compensated for freed slaves or lost property, and the fifth said that Congress could pass legislation to enforce any of the other provisions.

Since the president plays no role in either proposing or ratifying a constitutional amendment, Andrew Johnson could do nothing to prevent this amendment from becoming law. But three-quarters of state legislatures must ratify an amendment, and many in Congress were not certain how many states that was. Once again, whether or not the secessionist states were included in that number—and in the ratification process—depended on whether or not their secession was legal. Andrew Johnson's view that they were still part of the Union had been rejected when Southern congressmen were denied their seats in December 1865. Yet to ignore the eleven states entirely seemed wrong—they were, everyone agreed, going to rejoin the Union at *some* point. But there was no way that those states, with their white supremacist governments in place, would ratify an amendment that took away their own power.

Radicals came up with a workable—and likely illegal—solution. Confederate states would only be allowed to rejoin the Union if they ratified the Fourteenth Amendment. All that was left was to make sure that governments of those states would be willing to agree to an amendment that ensured equal rights and, almost certainly, gave African-American men the ability to vote. Equally important for the Radicals, the congressmen who would be seated from the readmitted South must be willing to vote to support their program for Reconstruction, which white supremacist state legislatures surely would not. And they did not. Of all the secessionist states, only Tennessee voted to ratify the amendment—which must have infuriated Andrew Johnson. The solution was clear.

If one could not persuade sitting governments to accept the amendment, it would be necessary to change the governments.

In March 1867, Congress passed "An Act to Provide for the More Efficient Government of the Rebel States," which quickly became known as the Reconstruction Act. The ten remaining secessionist states would be divided into five military districts, each commanded by an army general. These district commanders were to "protect all persons in their rights of person and property, to suppress insurrection, disorder, and violence, and to punish, or cause to be punished, all disturbers of the public peace and criminals." A commander could choose either regular courts or military tribunals to deal with the offenders.

Each of the ten states would also be required to "form a constitution . . . in conformity with the Constitution of the United States in all respects." State constitutions were to be drafted by "male citizens, twenty-one years old and upward, of whatever race, color, or previous condition." The resulting document would then need to be approved by Congress. When a state's constitution had been approved and a legislature formed, the state would be required to ratify the Fourteenth Amendment.

Andrew Johnson vetoed the bill almost the moment it was placed on his desk. He had complained to a newspaperman that whites "were being trodden under foot to protect niggers." Just as quickly, Congress overrode his veto.

Troops protecting freedmen after the Reconstruction Acts.

When none of the remaining ten secessionist states ratified the Fourteenth Amendment, the Radicals forced through
another Reconstruction Act, this one requiring the commanding general of each of the five military districts to register
every male twenty-one or over to vote on whether or not to
hold a state constitutional convention. The bill also gave
instructions on how the conventions would be held, how the
votes would be counted, and how the people counting
the votes would be protected, all under the security of the
army. Once again, Andrew Johnson vetoed the bill, and once
again the Radical Congress overrode him. In the history of

the United States to that point, never had there been a worse relationship between a president and Congress.

And Johnson was not without weapons of his own. As commander in chief, he was the man who appointed the commanders of the five military districts. Two expressed outright opposition to the Reconstruction Acts and two were more or less neutral. Only Philip Sheridan, in charge of the Louisiana and Texas district, actively aided the freedmen. Johnson replaced him.

But still, the Reconstruction Acts transformed the Confederacy. Union Leagues, which promoted African-American political activity, sprang up throughout the South. Freedmen registered to vote, asserted their civil and property rights, and attended schools sponsored by either the Freedmen's Bureau or private agencies. Blacks and whites traveled from the North to participate in the new South, some to make money, some because they believed deeply in equality for all people. To the white South, they were all "carpetbaggers," arriving only to line their pockets at the expense of a defeated nation.

Within months, thousands of black Americans, like Levi Nelson, gained access to the ballot box for the first time. Almost all registered as Republicans. In addition, military governments took the vote from large numbers of white Confederates. Anyone who had been deemed a "rebel" could be denied the vote. Almost all of these were Democrats. Under the watchful eye of the army, the state constitutional conventions were approved, African-Americans voting "aye" almost unanimously. New constitutions were then drafted and approved. The white supremacist governments were kicked out, replaced by Republican-controlled state legislatures whose goals aligned with only a small minority of the white population, but almost every black. Only then was the Fourteenth Amendment ratified and the former Confederate states readmitted to the Union.

But although whites in the South had been denied legal means to political power, they soon discovered that there were alternatives that could be every bit as effective as making speeches on street corners.

Illustration showing a woman, representing the South, being crushed under the weight of the carpetbaggers, who are protected by the Northern army of occupation.

1

THE KLAN—
NATHAN BEDFORD FORREST
AND MARY POLK BRANCH

IN DECEMBER 1865, AT almost the very moment the Radical
Republicans were refusing to seat congressmen from the
defeated Confederate states, a group of six young Confederate
war veterans, most college educated, was meeting in Pulaski,
Tennessee, a few miles north of the Alabama border. The town
had been named after Kazimierz Pułaski, the Polish nobleman
who had died heroically fighting for the Americans in the
Revolutionary War, and these men would spark a revolution of
a far different sort.

They had not met with that goal in mind, however. They
were simply interested in having some fun by dressing up in
elaborate disguises, inventing a series of secret passwords and
oaths of allegiance, calling each other a series of odd names,
and then galloping around town after dark, engaging in
pranks. They named the group Kuklux, evidently from the
Greek word *kuklos*, which means "ring" or "circle," although
there had been a group in ancient Greece with a similar name

that called itself Circle of the Moon. *Klan* seems to have been added simply because they liked the sound.

From the first, the targets of their "jokes" were local black residents. One of their early efforts involved a member of the group dressing in a white sheet and a frightening mask and then riding up to the home of a black family after midnight and demanding water. He would then seem to drink from the well bucket but would actually be pouring the water into a rubber tube hidden beneath his robe. He would demand more and more water until the black man watching him could not believe anyone could drink that much. The white man would thank the black man, say that he had not had a drink since he died on the battlefield at Shiloh, and gallop off into the darkness.

This all seemed like great fun until the white men realized that the freedmen genuinely believed the ghosts of dead Confederate soldiers were riding through the countryside. They also learned that they reminded the freedmen of the "slave patrols" that rode through the countryside at night before the Civil War, looking for runaways or any slaves that strayed out of their tumbledown cabins without permission. Beatings and whippings would follow.

Word spread quickly that freedmen were terrified of these strange "night riders," and new Klan groups popped up throughout the South. The outings soon turned more sinister. It was not long before the Kuklux began to use the terror that their rides provoked to "keep the freed slaves in line." The

TWO MEMBERS OF THE KU-KLUX KLAN IN THEIR DISGUISES.

An 1868 newspaper illustration of early Kuklux Klan members in their disguises.

whippings and beatings from the days of the slave patrols again became common.

In April 1867, just after Congress passed the Reconstruction Acts and the United States Army was sent as an occupying force into the South, a call went out to all the Klan chapters—there were now dozens and dozens—to send representatives to Nashville, Tennessee. At this meeting, what had been a loosely knit group of individual chapters became a disciplined organization, with rules, leaders, and a military-like chain of command. At the top of that chain would be the Grand Wizard. Chosen for the job was one of the most feared and respected of all the Confederate soldiers, a legend, the "Wizard of the Saddle," General Nathan Bedford Forrest. The title Grand Wizard was chosen because of Forrest's nickname.

Forrest had enlisted in the Confederate army as a private and risen to general in less than two years. He was a brilliant horseman, fearless fighter, ruthless with a saber or pistol, but most of all, he possessed perhaps the most brilliant military mind in the nation. Union General William Tecumseh Sherman described him as "the most remarkable man our civil war produced on either side," whose men "could travel one hundred miles in less time than ours can travel ten," and Ulysses Grant called him "that devil Forrest."

There were times when Forrest's cavalry seemed to be attacking in two or three places at once. He would strike at an opponent's weakness, then move to a different weak spot when the first was reinforced.

Nathan Bedford Forrest.

Forrest was almost supernaturally tough. At the Battle of Shiloh, where he was the last man wounded, he led a charge toward Union troops and found himself alone and surrounded in their midst. He fired his revolvers until they were empty and then slashed with his saber at the troops trying to pull him off his horse. Soon he was hit with a musket ball that lodged in his spine, an incredibly painful injury. Using his free hand, he grabbed a Union soldier by the shirt collar and pulled him off the ground, using the man as a shield as he rode through the enemy troops to safety. One week later, with no anesthesia to be had, an army surgeon removed the musket ball from Forrest's spine.

But Forrest was also a participant in one of the war's greatest atrocities. In April 1864, Forrest attacked Fort Pillow in

Henning, Tennessee, where a large part of the defending Union force were African-American soldiers.

Although Forrest later denied it, eyewitnesses—including those in Forrest's own command—insisted that after the Union garrison surrendered, he ordered all the black soldiers massacred. A Confederate soldier wrote to his sister, "The slaughter was awful. Words cannot describe the scene. The poor, deluded, negroes would run up to our men, fall upon their knees, and with uplifted hands scream for mercy, but they were ordered to their feet and then shot down. I, with several others, tried to stop the butchery, and at one time had partially succeeded, but General Forrest ordered them shot down like dogs and the carnage continued. Finally our men became sick of blood and the firing ceased." The incident, which would be an eerie precursor to the events to come in Colfax, did not result in any criminal charges against Forrest or any of his men.

An illustration of the slaughter at Fort Pillow.

The Kuklux, as it was still known, quickly began to function as a guerilla army, patrolling those areas of the South where United States troops either could not easily reach or that did not have enough people to justify stationing a unit there. Whipping and beating soon gave way to killing and the burning of homes. But to many white residents, the Klan became the force of law where the detested Yankees could not function. And that meant controlling the black population.

Mary Polk Branch was the widow of a Confederate general, a plantation owner, member of the best Southern gentry, and a first cousin to James K. Polk, the eleventh president of the United States. In 1912, she wrote the story of her life, *Memoirs of a Southern Woman*, in which she recounted stories of the Klan.

Then came Reconstruction days. It would have been very different if the negroes had been left to themselves, and not listened to the "carpet-baggers" who swarmed over the South, but by them they were incited to lawlessness and insult.

What could be done? There was no law! The Kuklux filled the needed want, and by thorough superstition awed the negroes into better behavior.

I have looked out in the moonlight, and seen a long procession wending their way slowly on the turnpike, in front of my house. Not a sound could be heard from the muffled feet of their horses, as in single file they moved in speechless silence—a spectral array clothed

Mary Polk Branch.

in white. No one knew who they were, whence they came, and what their object, but the negroes soon knew; and if there were excesses in their new-found liberty, crimes committed by them, they knew there would be a speedy retribution by these spectral visitants.

They effected a great good, but as good is often attended with evil, lawless men, who did not belong to the regular organization, disguised themselves as Kuklux.

**For instance, on my brother Lucius's plantation,
one night he was aroused by negroes from the quarter,
calling at his window, begging him to get up; that there
was, "A company of Kuklux at the quarter." He went at
once, and demanded what they wanted. They said:
"One of the negroes on the place has done a great deal
of mischief, and we have come to whip him." My brother
said: "I know him to be a good negro, and you cannot
whip him." "But we must!" "You cannot," said my
brother. "If you do it will be over my dead body, for I am
his natural protector." "Well, General, your life is too
valuable to be given for this negro's, so, as we do not
wish to kill you, we will go."**

But sometimes the Klansmen did not go, as an eyewitness
account by Thomas Burton makes clear. Burton was born a
slave in Kentucky in 1860, sent to school with the help of John
Fee, a white minister and founder of Berea College, and eventually became a doctor practicing in Indiana. Berea College
accepted students of all races, as did Reverend Fee's congregation. In 1872, while a young Thomas Burton sat in church, he
watched as Reverend Fee and Robert Jones, a member of the
congregation, paid the price for decency.

**The sermon had commenced when a mob of sixty
men with pistols and guns surrounded the house. One**

came in and said to Mr. Fee, "There are men here who wish you to stop and come out." He replied, "I am engaged in the exercise of a Constitutional right and a religious duty; please do not interrupt me," and preached on. The man went out, and soon two others returned and demanded that he come out. He preached on. They seized him and dragged him out, no resistance being made. Men with a rope swore they would hang him to the first tree unless he would promise to leave the county and never return. He replied, "I am in your hands; I would not harm you if you harm me; the responsibility is with you; I can make no pledge; duty to God and my country forbid." They swore they would duck him in the Kentucky River as long as life was in him unless he would promise to leave the county. He said: "I am a native of the State. I believe slavery is wrong. I am acting for the good of my country and all her people. You will know my motives at the judgment." He had proceeded but a few moments when one exclaimed, "We didn't come here to hear a sermon; let us do our work." They stripped Robert Jones naked, bent him down, and gave him thirty-three lashes with three sycamore rods. He was so injured that he could not walk the next day; but he made no pledges and did not leave. They said to Mr. Fee, "We will give you five hundred lashes if you do not leave the county and promise never to return." He knelt

down and said, "I will take my suffering; I can make no pledge." Later two lawyers were engaged to prosecute in behalf of him and Jones. The mob swore they would give five hundred lashes to any lawyer who would prosecute the cases. The grand jury never inquired into it. This is one of many such mobs through which Rev. John G. Fee went in those days.

Through terror and intimidation, the Klan in some areas operated as a shadow government or, as some called it, the Invisible Empire. They could not have much effect in the cities or in other areas where the army was a constant presence, but in the countryside, they could prevent newly freed black citizens from exercising the civil rights that the Radical Republicans in Congress had fought so hard to gain for them, the most important of which was the right to vote.

Success breeds imitators, and soon other groups of white supremacists formed, including one that operated in central Louisiana and was called the Knights of the White Camellia.

8

RECONSTRUCTION IN BLACK AND WHITE—HARRIET ANN JACOBS AND FRANK ALEXANDER MONTGOMERY

RECONSTRUCTION HAS BEEN ONE of the most debated periods in American history. For much of the twentieth century, it was thought of as a bungled experiment that tried to force people—both black and white—to behave in ways others thought they should, rather than in the way they wanted to on their own. Southern whites were made furious by having to accept black people into every area of their lives, and black people would have to take on responsibilities in business, government, and education that they had not been trained for. More recently, however, Reconstruction has been viewed as a noble attempt to correct a terrible wrong, where early promise was eventually wiped away because the effort was abandoned just as it was beginning to show success.

Supporters of each of these views look to accounts of those who experienced Reconstruction firsthand.

Harriet Ann Jacobs was born into slavery in North Carolina

in 1813. In 1835, to escape the sexual advances of her owner, Harriet ran away. She lived for seven years in hiding in a crawl space in the attic of her grandmother's shack. Finally, in 1842, she stowed away on a riverboat and reached Philadelphia. During the next twenty years, Harriet Jacobs became active in the abolition movement, helped start schools for young girls, and raised two children. In 1861, at the urging of Harriet Beecher Stowe, who had caused great upheaval with *Uncle Tom's Cabin*, Jacobs wrote a very successful novel of her own, *Incidents in the Life of a Slave Girl*, which was a fictionalized account of her own life.

After the war, Harriet Jacobs became one of the "carpet-baggers" white Southerners so hated. An account of some of her activities was published later:

Mrs. Harriet Jacobs was sent to Alexandria more than two years ago, by a Society of Friends in New York, to look after the Freedmen who were gathered there. Her first winter's service was a very hard one. Small-pox and other diseases made fearful havoc among the people; and all her energies were exhausted in caring for their physical needs.

Harriet Ann Jacobs.

**She has been unwearied in her labors, in provid-
ing orphan children with homes, in nursing the sick, in
assisting the able-bodied to find work, and in encour-
aging all in habits of industry and self-reliance. They
have established a school, and sent to the New
England Society for assistance in maintaining it. We
offered them a teacher, and sent them Miss Virginia
Lawton, a young colored woman of good education
and great worth of character (the grand-daughter of
one well known to the fashionable circles in Boston,
as the administrator of good things at weddings, chris-
tenings, parties, and other merry-makings), who has
taught there for a year. They have this autumn completed their school-house; and, as the school was too
large for Miss Lawton's care, we have sent them also
Mr. Banfield, a finely educated young man from New
Hampshire, who enters most heartily into the work.**

But Frank Alexander Montgomery, a lieutenant colonel in
the First Mississippi Cavalry, who would later serve as both a
member of the Mississippi legislature and a federal circuit
court judge, saw Reconstruction in a different light. In his
memoir, *Reminiscences of a Mississippian in Peace and War*,
Montgomery wrote that the Reconstruction Acts "provided for
a registration of negroes, with the avowed purpose of confer-
ring on them the right to vote and hold office, and at the same
time depriving a great many of the white people of these rights

[which] filled to overflowing the cup of bitterness the south was called upon to drink." Montgomery thought it "impossible to conceive that the ingenuity of hate could have devised anything which would have so humiliated the white people of the state as this cruel and unnecessary act, by which the former slave was placed upon a political equality with his master, in many cases superior to his master, for often the slave could vote while the master could not."

The source of the humiliation was obvious. "The people of the north did not understand the character of the negro; to them, or the vast majority, he was a white man with a black skin, while we of the south knew him to be not only an alien race, but so vastly inferior that no fit comparison now occurs to me. Whatever traits of character he had which raised him from a condition of barbarism he owed to his association with the white man, and to-day it is well known that if he were even now removed from this association he would relapse into the lowest grade of humanity."

Montgomery recalled watching with great bitterness as freedmen voted, the same act that would have caused Harriet Jacobs to rejoice. "The negroes stood in a long line, patiently waiting each till his turn should come, and had no more idea what he was doing or who he was voting for than 'the man in the moon' had."

But Colonel Montgomery's disgust or not, the presidential election of 1868 would, for the first time, allow men who had been slaves, most just three years earlier, to vote for the man who would lead their nation. By the time that vote occurred, however, the two great antagonists of Reconstruction had passed from the scene.

Andrew Johnson's departure was political. Tired of battling through his vetoes, the Radicals schemed to get him out of office. In 1867, Congress passed—over Johnson's veto—the Tenure of Office Act, which required the president to get approval from the Senate before replacing a cabinet member. Johnson was trying to get rid of Secretary of War Edwin Stanton, who he believed, correctly, was working against his Reconstruction policies. Stanton, of course, had been President Lincoln's secretary of war, and Johnson had kept him after the assassination as a gesture of goodwill. The Senate demanded Stanton remain in office. When Johnson fired Stanton anyway, Congress, with Thaddeus Stevens as a driving force, began a process called impeachment, which would remove the president from office. Ordinarily, that would leave the presidency to the vice president, but since that office was vacant, next in line was a Radical Republican, Benjamin Wade of Ohio, president pro tempore of the Senate. (Succession has since been changed so that the Speaker of the House of Representatives is now third in line.)

Impeachment is simply an indictment, a formal legal accusation, that is made in the House of Representatives by a majority vote. If the president is impeached, he must then stand trial in the Senate, where a two-thirds vote is required

HARPER'S WEEKLY.

A JOURNAL OF CIVILIZATION.

L. XI.—No. 568.]   NEW YORK, SATURDAY. NOVEMBER 16, 1867.   [SINGLE COPIES TEN CENTS. $4.00 PER YEAR IN ADVANCE.

Entered According to Act of Congress, in the Year 1867, by Harper & Brothers, in the Clerk's Office of the District Court for the Southern District of New York.

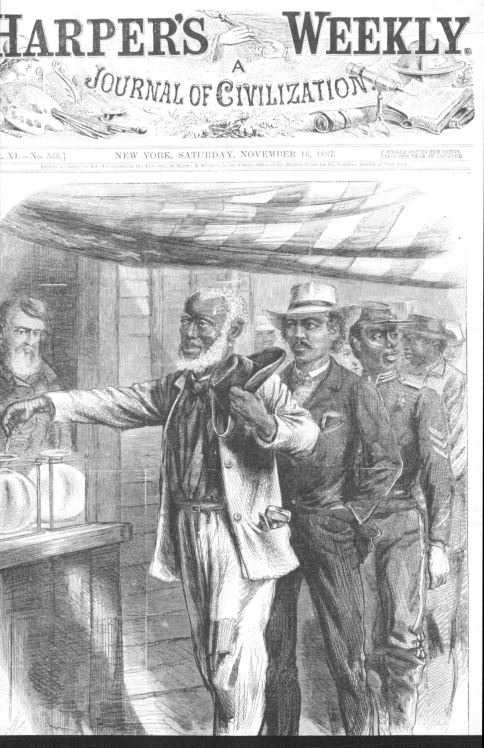

"The First Vote." An 1867 magazine cover.

to convict. Andrew Johnson was the first president ever impeached. That occurred on February 24, 1868, when a resolution sponsored by Thaddeus Stevens and John Bingham passed the House by a vote of 126–47.

The trial, however, did not go as the Radicals had planned. Despite having enough Republicans in the Senate to reach the necessary two-thirds to convict President Johnson and remove him from office, the Radicals fell one vote short. Although Radicals applied immense pressure, some Republicans refused to vote for an action they saw as unfair, unnecessary, and possibly illegal. Radicals tried a number of times, but in late May 1868, they gave up. Andrew Johnson got to finish out his term—which had only nine months to run—but any remaining political power he had was gone. Republicans were fully in control of the government.

But Thaddeus Stevens would not be able to share in that control for very long. Only three months after the not guilty verdict was posted, Stevens was dead. He had been ill for some time, but his death came suddenly, at midnight on August 11, 1868.

Stevens aroused the same strong feelings in death as he had in life. Philadelphia's *Evening Telegraph* devoted its entire front page to the departed lion of Reconstruction and said, "He lived and breathed and had his whole being in the strife of public life . . . While the bitterness of the opposition which he excited and courted has rarely been equaled, he nevertheless commanded the respect and admiration of almost everyone

Ticket to Andrew Johnson's impeachment trial.

who was arrayed against him. His most commanding qualities were fiery zeal and unquestionable honesty of purpose, and these are qualities which never fail to win the admiration and respect of opponents. Nor could any man question the generosity of his heart, or his sincere devotion to the interests of his fellow-men."

But many newspapers were less praising. The *New York Times*, in an editorial, called Stevens the "Evil Genius of the Republican Party" whose manner "tended to develop the intolerant spirit from which the party suffered." He was, according to the *Times*, "defiant, despotic, and in all things irritating." The *Brooklyn Daily Eagle* added that "intolerance of opposition . . . alone enabled so ill-informed and narrow minded a man as the late Thaddeus Stevens to be the leader of a party."

Surprisingly, Stevens himself also had a less than complimentary view of his own achievements. On his deathbed, he told a reporter, "I have achieved nothing in Congress . . . Some of the papers call me 'Leader of the House.' I only laugh at them. I lead them, yes; but they never follow me or do as I want them until public opinion has sided with me."

But Stevens's self-appraisal was not shared among the general public. When he lay in state in the Capitol, he attracted a stream of mourners outstripped only by Abraham Lincoln. And intolerant though he might have been, it is necessary to ask how the struggle for equal rights would have survived

Thaddeus Stevens and John Bingham prosecuting Andrew Johnson before the Senate.

without him. Although he may have badly blundered in the impeachment of Andrew Johnson, he was most responsible for removing Johnson's white supremacist postwar state legislatures and eliminating the Black Codes. That his victory was temporary does not mean Stevens failed. It simply means that the nation did not have more men like Thaddeus Stevens when it most needed them.

9

AN ISLAND FOR FREEDMEN— COLFAX

NOTHING ABOUT COLFAX WAS ordinary—not its name, its history, how it was governed, or what it had been before.

Andrew Johnson did not run for reelection in 1868. Instead, the Democrats nominated a proslavery Northerner, Governor Horatio Seymour of New York. Seymour ran a spirited campaign and made a decent showing, but his candidacy was doomed from the start. As his opponent, Republicans nominated one of the most popular men in the nation—or at least in the northern part of the nation—General Ulysses S. Grant. For vice president, Republicans nominated the Speaker of the House of Representatives, Indiana's Schuyler Colfax.

Although Seymour lost the popular vote by only 300,000 of the almost six million cast, Grant won twenty-six states to Seymour's eight for an electoral vote margin of 214–80. The electoral vote might have been closer except for Grant's 41–16 margin in the South, which was enabled, of course, by the overwhelming support of freedmen for the Republican Party.

The only two Southern states that Grant did not win were Georgia and Louisiana.

Not surprisingly, the Democrats did particularly well in those areas of Louisiana farther from the major cities and therefore the army. One of the areas of a strong white vote was Rapides Parish, on the Red River about two hundred miles northwest of New Orleans. Unlike in most areas of white domination, however, the largest landowner in Rapides, in fact one of the largest in the entire state, was a plantation owner named William S. Calhoun. Not only did Willie Calhoun hold racial views far more progressive than most of his white neighbors, he was active in the Republican Party, was a member of the Louisiana legislature, and did his best to ensure that his former slaves, now freedmen, voted in the election.

Willie Calhoun was an odd man with an even odder upbringing for backwoods Louisiana. He was not born in the state, or even in the United States, but rather in Paris, France, in 1835, while his family was on an extended vacation there. His father, Meredith, had inherited seven thousand acres and, before Willie was born, had purchased seven thousand more. In all, Willie Calhoun would inherit more than twenty square miles of property, stretching seven miles down the Red River in Louisiana. Meredith divided the land into four plantations. A small complex of buildings on the riverfront was called Calhoun's Landing. Meredith Calhoun was a diehard Democrat and white supremacist, who owned more than seven hundred slaves. He was thought to be so cruel that a rumor later circulated that he had been the model for Simon Legree, the vicious taskmaster in *Uncle Tom's Cabin*. The elder Calhoun also published a Democratic newspaper and was at one point elected to the Louisiana senate.

Soon after Willie was born, the family returned from Europe, and just after that, he suffered a broken back in a carriage accident. It would leave Willie stunted and deformed for the rest of his life. In an attempt to cure his injuries, his parents sent him back to France for an extended stay with French doctors, judged superior to any in the United States. Although the French doctors were not successful, French culture must have left its mark, because Willie Calhoun would become an enlightened, tolerant man who was determined to make amends for the sin of slavery committed by his father.

Willie Calhoun was in no way weak. He maintained his commitment to the Union when all about him preached secession, and he would eventually endure insults, threats, and attempts to take his property from him. After the war, he became the one landowner in Rapides Parish committed to making Reconstruction work.

And in 1869, he decided to do that by creating a parish in which freedmen would be in the majority. So he sponsored a bill in the Louisiana legislature to create such a parish out of his own vast holdings which, in honor of the new Republican president, he named Grant Parish. For the parish seat, he would take the name of the new vice president and call it

Colfax. There wasn't really a town where Colfax would be situated, so one of Willie Calhoun's stables was hastily converted into a "courthouse," where the parish council would meet, cases would be tried, and important records would be stored.

Although most of Grant Parish's officials would be white Republicans, an exception was the captain of the local Louisiana state militia unit. He was William Ward, a former slave from Virginia who had been trained as a carpenter but escaped during the war to join the Union army. He was discharged after the war but reenlisted in 1867 and was stationed in Mississippi. He was discharged again in 1870 when he was diagnosed with tuberculosis, and moved with his wife to Grant Parish. Ward was a bitter, hard-driven man who disliked most white men in the South as much as they disliked him. In an effort he thought would promote racial peace, Louisiana's governor, Republican Henry Clay Warmoth, had instructed Ward that the militia unit be half-white and half-black, and even contain some former Confederate soldiers. But Ward refused and the Grant Parish militia contained only black members.

From its founding, politics in Grant Parish were tense, chaotic, and often violent. White against black, Democrat against Republican, even moderate Republican against Radical Republican, would all be the cause of disruption and death, finally ending in a horrific mass murder that shocked and divided America.

The very creation of the new political entity infuriated the surrounding white majority, but it was the appointment of two officials, both white, both army veterans—one Union, one Confederate—that set the stage for the race war to come. Each had been chosen in part because he had refused to back down after repeated threats from local night riders.

The Klan and the White Camellia had experienced a good deal of success in frightening local freedmen away from the voting booth in Rapides Parish. There had been whippings and beatings, and one local black businessman, Hal Frazier, had been gunned down at his sawmill by two white men in broad daylight. It was just that sort of activity these new parish officials had been charged to stop.

The Union man was the new parish sheriff, Delos White, who had been born in Flushing, New York, served in the cavalry, and came south after the war as an agent for the Freedmen's Bureau. In that job, he had shown no tolerance for mistreatment of the local black population, and time and again had arrested whites accused of crimes against freedmen and had them hauled off to New Orleans for trial before a military court. In his reports to the Freedmen's Bureau, he wrote that local blacks were "sober and industrious," and that their "moral character" was superior to that of local whites. Just weeks after his appointment, two armed men accosted White on the road and demanded that he leave within twenty-four hours. White ignored them.

The Confederate was William B. Phillips, the new parish judge. He was Alabama born, also a former cavalryman, but had come to the Red River as a Republican, proclaiming himself a great friend of the freedmen, which he would prove if they elected him to office. But many thought Phillips to be simply an opportunist, someone who was taking advantage of the freedmen's inexperience with politics and would say whatever it took to advance his career. Democrats in particular hated him, especially after he began living openly with a black woman, with whom he had a son. Phillips received the same demands to leave and, like Delos White, ignored them.

Eventually, Governor Warmoth realized that his goal of racial tolerance could never be met with two men so despised by the white population, so he replaced White and Phillips with men of more moderate reputation. Phillips and White immediately organized a Radical group to oppose Warmoth and called on the freedmen to support them. One of those who did was William Ward, whose militia unit was the only legally armed group in the parish. Of course, white supremacists, most of whom had fought in the Civil War, were both better armed and better trained.

In the elections of 1870, Phillips got himself elected to be once again parish judge, and Delos White also gained a spot in parish government. The new sheriff, however, was Alfred Shelby, an illiterate, hard-drinking brute of a man, one of whose close associates was a local landowner, James Hadnot.

Hadnot was one of the area's most avowed white supremacists, and one of the most feared by freedmen. It was generally known—and Hadnot made little attempt to hide it—that either he personally or others in his employ were responsible for a good deal of the whippings and beatings, and also for the threats against voting. One Hadnot associate had ridden up to a group of freedmen on their way to vote and said he would shoot on the spot anyone who did not turn around. All of them did.

Judge Phillips intended to put a stop to such behavior and instructed Shelby to arrest those identified by freedmen as the perpetrators. Shelby, who boasted of having fought in the war, but probably did not, simply refused to do his job. Eventually, relations between Shelby and Phillips and White became so strained that Shelby began to threaten their lives and was even reported to have offered a black man one hundred dollars to kill them. But Phillips and White had faced down threats before.

On the night of September 25, 1871, White and Phillips, who were by then sharing a house, better for mutual defense, were awakened by the noise of men and horses outside. Then they realized their house had been set on fire. They jumped from their beds and made for the door, but the exits had been blocked by guards armed with double-barreled shotguns. Glancing through the window, they saw a mob of fifty men. Remaining in the house meant roasting to death, so Delos White flung open the front door, only to come face-to-face with Deputy Sheriff Christopher Columbus "C. C." Nash.

Unlike Alfred Shelby, Nash had definitely fought in the war. He had been an officer who had been present for the war's opening salvo, the First Battle of Bull Run, and then in many other battles, including Gettysburg. He had been taken prisoner later in 1863 and lived out the war in a cold, filthy prison on Lake Erie, where the prisoners were forced to trap and cook rats in order to get enough to eat. He was a cold, hard man with a thick black beard and coal-black eyes. As soon as the door flew open, he shot Delos White with both barrels, killing him instantly. Others opened fire, and William Phillips fell to the ground as well, seemingly dead. The mob left, but not before lighting a torch on top of a twelve-foot pole on which was tacked a copy of a speech Phillips had given four years before.

But William Phillips was still alive. He had only pretended to be dead, hoping the mob would leave, which they did. More than that, Phillips had seen the leaders of the mob, including C. C. Nash and Alfred Shelby. Still recovering from his wounds, Phillips took a boat to New Orleans and there swore out warrants against Shelby, Nash, and six others, a mix of Democrats and what had become known as "conservative Republicans"— that is, people who had joined the party but had not given up white supremacist views.

Governor Warmoth did not act on the warrants but did ship modern Enfield rifles to William Ward with instructions that they not be issued to the militia without authorization. The sight of armed black men marching to arrest white men accused of murder was not likely to calm what had become an explosive situation in Colfax.

But William Ward had no intention of sitting by until some politician said it was all right for him to arrest white murderers. He promptly rounded up all eight, placed them under guard, and sent word for a federal marshal to come to Colfax to transfer them to New Orleans. When the marshal arrived, however, rather than remove the prisoners, he had to wait while a Louisiana judge friendly to the defendants decided if the arrest had been legal. With Phillips and Ward listening in the courtroom—the converted stable—the judge refused to release the prisoners to the marshal, and said instead he would try the case himself.

Phillips and Ward were furious, but it seemed they would be helpless to do anything. But then Ward heard a steamboat approaching. He went outside and ordered his militia—armed with the Enfields—into the courtroom, bayonets fixed. When the judge protested, Ward is reported to have said, "Damn the court," and marched the prisoners to the waiting steamboat for transfer to New Orleans.

Ward then summoned federal marshals from New Orleans and proceeded to arrest any white man who had been implicated in "violating the civil rights" of freedmen. These, according to a number of laws passed by Congress, known as "Enforcement Acts," were federal crimes and would be tried in federal courts. Enforcement Acts could not be applied to strictly state crimes, like murder, unless the murder could be shown to have been racially motivated and therefore had denied the victim "equal protection of the laws," as defined in the Fourteenth Amendment. All the same, the Enforcement Acts were drawn to cover a wide range of activities that had previously been only in the power of state governments to control.

Whites hated this broad, sweeping power of arrest and hated Ward for employing it. They complained to Governor Warmoth that Ward had begun a "reign of terror." But Ward pressed on, his militia even gunning down a suspect whom they said resisted arrest. Eventually, Warmoth had no choice but to have Ward relieved of his command and the militia unit officially disbanded. But officially did not mean that Ward and his men stopped thinking of themselves as the law in Grant Parish. They did, however, lose the Enfields.

The Radicals were not having much better luck in New Orleans. Although Albert Shelby and C. C. Nash had been held in prison without bail—the others had made bail and returned home—when a federal grand jury met to consider the charges, they found the evidence was not sufficient to bring charges against the two men. They were then free to return home, which in February 1872 they did, in bad humor. A "grand jury" is a panel of citizens whose role is to decide if there is enough evidence to indict someone accused of a crime. If they decide there is, the accused is then tried before a "petit jury"—a regular jury—which decides guilt or innocence. In the impeachment of Andrew Johnson, the House of Representatives acted as a grand jury and the Senate as a petit jury.

There was occasional violence on both sides, but no

incidents were serious enough to justify stationing an army unit in Colfax. The Radicals continued to send word to New Orleans that they were living under threat of death, but every time a detachment of soldiers was sent up the Red River, they found that the Radicals were at least as responsible for the incidents—perhaps more—as were the white men they were complaining about.

By summer 1872, Governor Warmoth concluded that his dream of racial harmony through a tolerant and forgiving Republican Party was hopeless. That decision set the stage for one of the most corrupt elections in American history—no small feat—and eventually led directly to the slaughter at Colfax.

FRAUD RUNS WILD— SAMUEL MCENERY AND WILLIAM KELLOGG

AFTER THE ELECTIONS OF 1868, Republicans realized that their position as the dominant political party was in danger. Ulysses Grant's big win in the Electoral College disguised what was a surprisingly close race in the popular vote. And three Southern states—Texas, Virginia, and Mississippi—had not participated because they had not yet been readmitted to the Union.

Grant's victory had come about almost entirely as a result of freedmen. Without the black vote, nearly exclusively Republican in the South, Horatio Seymour likely would have been president. That support would become even more necessary in 1872, when the three absent Southern states would participate. But Democrats had made big gains in state legislatures in the South and it was not impossible that they might find ways to disqualify freedmen from voting. In addition, the Democratic Party was gaining power in the North, where many people had grown tired of the time and money spent to protect the rights of black Americans. It became vital, then, for Republicans to ensure that African-Americans could continue to vote and not risk their being denied the vote by a state whose legislature had fallen into Democratic hands. Once again, they would turn to the Constitution as the solution.

With John Bingham leading the way once more, Republicans in Congress introduced an amendment that would prohibit denying anyone the vote on the basis of their race or "previous condition of servitude," the standard code phrase for *slave*. Bingham also wanted to guarantee that freedmen would not be prevented from voting by any little tricks that Southern—or even Northern—Democrats might come up with. His original proposal banned literacy tests, a poll tax—requiring a fee in order to vote—education requirements, property ownership, or place of birth as reasons for denying someone the right to register to vote. But these went too far for Democrats, and even for Republicans none too thrilled at seeing their party dominated by black skin. So only a bare-bones version of the amendment was finally agreed to, with no mention of any of the ways those who wished to deny black people the vote could do so. Each of these devices would be used extensively by Southern states in the coming years. Still, in late February 1869, just one week before President Grant would be sworn in, Congress approved the amendment with the required two-thirds vote, agreeing, at least in principle, that the right to vote should not be based on the color of one's skin.

Getting the amendment ratified by three-quarters of the

states, however, promised to be a serious challenge. Opposition was not just on racial grounds—many women who were fiercely campaigning for the right to vote themselves were furious that they had been left out. But with Radical governments still in charge in many states—at least for the moment—the amendment got a boost. To nudge those Southern states that might have second thoughts, Congress passed bills—which President Grant signed—requiring Virginia, Mississippi, Texas, and Georgia to ratify the amendment to regain their seats in Congress. It took almost an entire year, but in early February 1870, the required twenty-eight states had ratified, and the Fifteenth Amendment became law.

Those who had been in favor of enshrining black voting rights in the Constitution cheered—never again would a black person be denied the right to vote because of the color of his skin. (Of course, the Supreme Court would have something to say about that, and once again, John Bingham had correctly predicted the future.) Opponents were furious: In yet another law, black people had been elevated to equality with what was to their mind the superior white race, able to pollute state and local governments, the halls of Congress, and perhaps one terrible day, even the presidency itself.

The last thing Louisiana needed in 1870 was another complication to its political situation. The shifting alliances, filled with impeachment, power grabs, arrests, and accusations of betrayal might have been pulled out of a bizarre comedy if the stakes were not so serious.

"All Men Free and Equal."

THE XVTH AMENDMENT PROCLAIMED.

MESSAGE TO CONGRESS.—PROCLAMATION OF THE PRESIDENT.

Proclaim Liberty throughout all the Land, to all the Inhabitants thereof.

> Oh ! not yet
> May'st thou, O Freedom, close thy lids,
> In slumber; for thine enemy never sleeps,
> And thou must watch and combat, till the day
> Of the new earth and heaven.

To all to whom these presents come—Greeting:

Know ye that the Congress of the United States, on or about the 27th day of February, in the year one thousand eight hundred and sixty-nine, passed a resolution in the words and figures following to wit :

A resolution proposing an amendment to the Constitution of the United States.

Resolved, By the Senate and House of Representatives of the United States of America in Congress assembled, two-thirds of both Houses concurring, that the following article be proposed to the Legislatures of the several States as an amendment to the Constitution of the United States, which, when ratified by three-fourths of said Legislatures, shall be valid as part of the Constitution, namely :

ARTICLE 15, SECTION 1. The rights of citizens of the United States to vote, shall not be denied or abridged by the United States, or by any State, on account of race, color, or previous condition of servitude.

SECTION 2. The Congress shall have power to enforce this article by appropriate legislation.

And further, That it appears from the official document on file in this Department that the Amendment to the Constitution of the United States, proposed as aforesaid, has been ratified by the Legislatures of the States of—

NORTH CAROLINA,	CONNECTICUT,	MISSOURI,
WEST VIRGINIA,	FLORIDA,	MISSISSIPPI,
MASSACHUSETTS,	ILLINOIS,	OHIO,
WISCONSIN,	INDIANA,	IOWA,
MAINE,	NEW YORK,	KANSAS,
LOUISIANA,	NEW HAMPSHIRE,	MINNESOTA,
MICHIGAN,	NEVADA,	RHODE ISLAND,
SOUTH CAROLINA,	VERMONT,	NEBRASKA,
PENNSYLVANIA,	VIRGINIA,	TEXAS.
ARKANSAS,	ALABAMA,	

In all 29 States.

And further, That the States whose Legislatures have so ratified the said proposed amendment constitute three-fourths of the whole number of States in the United States.

And further, That it appears from an official document, on file in this Department, that the Legislature of the State of New York has since passed resolutions claiming to withdraw the said ratification of the said amendment which has been made by the Legislature of that State, and of which official notice has been filed in this Department.

And further, That it appears from an official document, on file in this Department, that the Legislature of Georgia has by resolution ratified the said proposed amendment.

Now, therefore, be it known, That I, Hamilton Fish, Secretary of State, of the United States, by virtue and in pursuance of the second section of the Act of Congress, approved the 20th day of April, in the year 1818, entitled "An act to provide for the publication of the laws of the United States and for other purposes," do hereby certify that the Amendment aforesaid has become valid to all intents and purposes as a part of the Constitution of the United States.

In testimony whereof, I have hereunto set my hand and caused the seal of the Department of State to be affixed.

Done at the City of Washington, this thirteenth day of March, in the year of our Lord, one thousand eight hundred and seventy, and of the independence of the United States the ninety-fourth.

HAMILTON FISH.

MESSAGE FROM THE PRESIDENT.

To the Senate and House of Representatives :

It is unusual to notify the two Houses of Congress by message of the promulgation, by the proclamation of the Secretary of state, of the ratification of a Constitutional Amendment. In view, however, of the vast importance of the Fifteenth Amendment of the Constitution, this day declared a part of that revered instrument, I deem a departure from the usual custom justifiable. A measure which makes at once four millions of people voters, who were heretofore declared by the highest tribunal in the land not citizens of the United States, nor eligible to become so, with the assertion that at the time of the Declaration of Independence the opinion was fixed and universal—in the civilized portion of the white race, regarded as an axiom in morals as well as in politics—that "black men had no rights which white men were bound to respect," is indeed a measure of grander importance than any other one act of the kind from the foundation of our free Government to the present time. Institutions like ours, in which all power is derived directly from the people, must depend mainly upon their intelligence, patriotism, and industry. I call the attention, therefore, of the newly-enfranchised race to the importance of their striving, in every honorable manner, to make themselves worthy of their new privilege. To the race more favored heretofore by our laws, I would say, withhold no legal privilege of advancement to the new citizen. The framers of our Constitution firmly believed that a republican form of government could not endure without intelligence and education generally diffused among the people. The Father of his Country in his Farewell Address, uses this language : " Promote, then, as a matter of primary importance, institutions for the general diffusion of knowledge. In proportion as the structure of the Government gives force to public opinion, it is essential that public opinion should be enlightened." In his first annual Message to Congress the same views were forcibly presented, and are again urged in his eighth Message.

I repeat, that the adoption of the Fifteenth Amendment to the Constitution completes the greatest civil change, and constitutes the most important event that has occurred since the nation came into life. The change will be beneficial in proportion to the heed that is given to the urgent recommendations of Washington. If these recommendations were important then, with a population of but a few millions, how much more important now, with a population of forty millions, and increasing in a rapid ratio ! I would therefore call upon Congress to take all the means within their constitutional power to promote and encourage popular education throughout the country, and upon the people everywhere to see to it that all who possess and exercise political rights shall have the opportunity to acquire the knowledge which will make their share in the Government a blessing and not a danger. By such means only can the benefits contemplated by this amendment to the Constitution be secured.

U. S. GRANT.

Executive Mansion, March 30, 1870.

HAMILTON FISH, *Secretary of State of the United States.*

In all of the States engaged in the Rebellion negroes are already recognized as voters by virtue of the terms of the Reconstruction acts, and the acceptance of these by the States in question. In most of the other States, however, their exercise of the franchise has either been denied or limited by property or other qualifications. The following table shows approximately the number of voters thus added to the voting population in each of these States :

States.	Negro Population.	New Voters.
California	4,086	681
Connecticut	8,627	1,438
Delaware	21,027	3,604
Illinois	7,628	1,271
Indiana	11,428	1,805
Iowa	1,069	178
Kentucky	236,167	39,561
Maine	1,327	221
Maryland	171,131	28,522
Massachusetts	9,662	1,600
Michigan	6,799	1,128
Minnesota	233	93
New Hampshire	494	82
New Jersey	25,336	4,226
New York	49,005	8,167
Ohio	36,673	6,112
Oregon	128	21
Pennsylvania	56,849	9,475
Rhode Island	3,952	659
Vermont	709	118
Wisconsin	1,171	195

Printed for AMOS G. BEMAN.

The Fifteenth Amendment.

104

Everyone was involved in the madness, none more than Governor Warmoth. So determined were Democrats to be rid of the Prince of the Carpetbaggers, as they termed him, that they hatched a plot to have his supporters in the legislature taken on a riverboat excursion so that those left could impeach him. Warmoth was in fact locked up for a time. He insisted that impeachment was not his enemies' true goal—that rather they intended to have him assassinated. His lieutenant governor, a "free Creole of color" named P. B. S. Pinchback, moved back and forth between the two camps—and for a time served as acting governor—and would eventually accuse Warmoth of bribery. Warmoth, on the other hand, abandoned his lieutenant governor in 1871 and supported General Joseph R. West—another carpetbagger—for election to the United States Senate, a seat Pinchback desperately wanted. West won.

Warmoth had made no shortage of enemies in his life, and one of them was the president of the United States. During the Civil War, after being wounded at the Battle of Vicksburg, Warmoth had criticized Grant's tactics in a newspaper interview. Grant had him thrown out of the army, but Warmoth had petitioned personally to President Lincoln and won reinstatement. Warmoth had done his best to regain President Grant's favor by supporting the president's brother-in-law for an important position in New Orleans.

By the time it came to choose candidates to run in the 1872 governor's race, there had been so many changes of sides and so many odd maneuvers—including an instance in which

P. B. S. Pinchback, the first African-American governor, if only for a few days.

Warmoth's supporters were blocked by troops from entering their own party's convention—that chaos seemed inevitable. As it turned out to be.

By summer 1872, the Republican Party had officially split. A group calling themselves Liberal Republicans nominated New York newspaper publisher Horace Greeley to run against President Grant. The Greeley backers were only liberal to distance themselves from the Radicals that they claimed Grant supported. While the liberals claimed to be in favor of equal rights, they were also in favor of withdrawing the army from the Southern states, which Grant opposed. They were, therefore, appealing to Democrats who decided to throw their support to Greeley in the November election. It would not matter. Greeley lost badly and then died before the electoral votes had been submitted. He thus became the only major party candidate in American history to receive no electoral votes.

Henry Warmoth decided that the split in the Republican Party was his opportunity. He abandoned Grant and the regular Republicans and instead called for a Liberal Republican convention to nominate candidates for state offices. Once again trying to recruit moderate Democrats, and even possibly black Republicans, the party's motto was Justice to All Races, Creeds, and Political Opinions. But African-Americans understood that by All Races, Warmoth meant whites. They also had no intention of joining Democrats against the party that had done its best to ensure equal rights. Getting nowhere

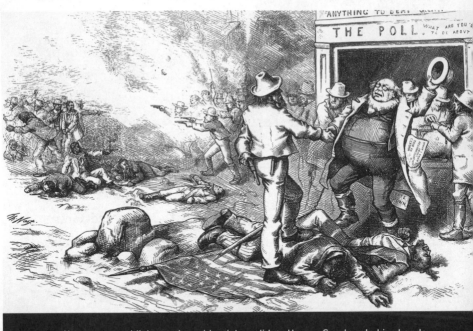

Newspaper publisher and presidential candidate Horace Greeley shaking hands with the ghost of John Wilkes Booth over Abraham Lincoln's body, while Redeemers murder freedmen. Greeley would have ended Reconstruction.

with black voters, Warmoth turned instead to more radical Democrats. They agreed to join with the Liberal Republicans if Warmoth agreed not to run for reelection. Warmoth had little choice but to comply and so they put forth a Fusion ticket with John D. McEnery, a white supremacist Democrat, as their candidate for governor. The Fusionists supported Greeley for president, which cemented Warmoth's break with both Grant and the regular Republicans.

McEnery had the perfect credentials for former Confederates. He had begun the Civil War as a captain in the Louisiana infantry, was promoted to a major in March 1862, and two months after to lieutenant colonel. He fought bravely throughout the war. Even better, after he was elected to the Louisiana legislature in 1866, Union officials refused to let him take office because he would not renounce his pro-Confederate views.

To oppose McEnery, the Grant Republicans nominated William Pitt Kellogg, a sitting Louisiana United States senator. Kellogg, one of the first carpetbaggers, was reviled by Democrats, particularly the more extreme former Confederates. Even many Republicans disliked him. At first, P. B. S. Pinchback, now on his own after his break with Warmoth, wanted to oppose Kellogg and run for governor on his own, but was eventually persuaded to support Kellogg in return for being placed on the ticket as a candidate for Congress. Securing Pinchback's support made Kellogg far more acceptable to many Republicans, in particular the freedmen, whose votes would almost certainly decide the election.

William Pitt Kellogg.

In Grant Parish, the two sides were equally extreme. The Fusion nominee for sheriff was none other than C. C. Nash, now a hero to many whites for gunning down Delos White and getting away with it. The Republican candidate for state representative was William Ward, who frightened whites as much as Nash terrified blacks. His opponent would be the arch white supremacist James Hadnot.

The election, held on November 4, 1872, was one of the strangest in United States history. Even today, Louisiana historians describe it as "unique" or "weird." In a nation where voter fraud was hardly unknown, this election set a new standard. It is not possible, even now, to determine which candidate actually garnered more votes. Ballot boxes were stuffed or thrown in a nearby river; people voted more than once, often in different locations; many votes were cast by men already dead; votes were counted more than once or not at all—almost every means of perpetrating fraud at the ballot box was indulged in with gusto by both sides. In Grant Parish, the process was so obviously corrupt that an official vote count was never submitted at all. There, as in the rest of the state, both sides claimed victory.

The trouble officially began about a week after election day, when the official Louisiana elections board was to meet to certify the votes and declare a winner. The problem was that there was no official board but rather two boards, one for each side, each claiming to have the legal right to declare the winner. After one of the boards, which had been approved by a federal judge, declared Grant and Kellogg the victors, Henry Warmoth, still governor, called a special session of the Louisiana legislature to abolish that board and appoint a new one. On December 4, 1872, the new board, predictably, declared Greeley and McEnery as the winners. With that announcement, some of the Fusion candidates in Grant Parish, including the new sheriff, C. C. Nash, but not James Hadnot, were sworn in, given their commissions, and sent home to assume their duties.

The Kellogg faction then went to federal court and persuaded the judge—a Grant appointee—to declare its decision void. Federal marshals were dispatched to seal the building where the votes were kept and to prevent Warmoth and McEnery supporters from entering. On December 6, the same judge declared Warmoth's new board illegal and declared Kellogg the winner. From there, with the main antagonists now Warmoth and Pinchback—the governor and lieutenant governor, at least on paper—each side tried legal mancuvers with the support of friendly judges.

McEnery's forces, convinced they had won, although it is not clear how they could have been so certain, decided to send a delegation to Washington to meet with President Grant. McEnery himself headed the "committee of one hundred." Grant refused to meet with them. "Thus Grant too," wrote Louis Nardini, Sr., a Louisiana historian in 1962, "our eighteenth President of the United States, because he turned a deaf ear to justice and in defiance of the Bill of Rights by not granting an audience to these men, was partly responsible for what was to follow."

On January 13, 1873, Henry Warmoth's term expired. Usually, the end of a term would be marked by the inauguration of a successor. This time, in the spirit of the election just completed, there were two inaugurations. (There were two sets of presidential electors as well. The Electoral College solved the problem by not accepting either one.)

With the support of federal judges and the army, Kellogg became the only one of the two governors recognized by the federal government in Washington, DC. While Kellogg, of course, did not recognize Nash and the other Grant Parish Fusionists as genuine officeholders, fearing violence, he did not at first move to install Republicans in those offices.

And McEnery was not yet beaten. He and his fellow Fusionists formed a competing government that met in the Odd Fellows Hall in New Orleans. The problem for McEnery, however, was that he could not collect taxes or otherwise raise revenue. As March began, his situation had grown dire, so in a last desperate attempt to win the governorship, McEnery called on his supporters to mount an armed attack on the Metropolitan Police, and then to take over the government by force. Known as the First Battle of Liberty Place—there would be a similar attempt the following year—McEnery's coup failed. His mob lost their taste for a fight when faced with the well-armed, well-disciplined police. After a police official threatened to call the army as well, after a couple of random shots, the Fusionists left.

In Grant Parish, James Hadnot, Sheriff Nash, and other Fusionists could not help but realize that McEnery's attempt at violent overthrow would almost certainly result in Governor Kellogg either removing them from office—in Nash's case—or refusing to seat them—in Hadnot's. They decided to negotiate. They sent two local lawyers, both Democrats, to New Orleans to meet with the governor and offer him a deal. If Kellogg would agree to allow the Fusionists to either take or keep their offices, they would guarantee peace in Grant Parish. Otherwise, there would almost certainly be bloodshed.

Incredibly, Kellogg agreed. The murderer of Delos White would remain as sheriff, and the man who had done as much as anyone to prompt it would become state representative. Democrats would occupy most of the other key offices as well, with a token Republican or two given only unimportant posts.

When the lawyers returned to Colfax with the news, Republicans exploded, none more so than William Ward. In their view, they had risked their lives simply to run for office in a place where opponents were perfectly content to kill those who crossed them. There could be no greater betrayal. Ward rushed to New Orleans to confront Kellogg and demand to know how he could have approved a murderer as sheriff and a hardened white supremacist and reputed Klan leader for state representative—the job he had been filling—over those who had worked hard to ensure a Republican victory. Kellogg claimed he had not known of the Delos White affair—he had been in Washington—and agreed to revise his list of officeholders. Under no circumstances, he promised, would Christopher Columbus Nash be sheriff. And of course William Ward would be state representative. Ward immediately headed back to Colfax to supervise the change in parish officials.

Now it was Hadnot and Nash's turn to scream betrayal. When Republicans showed up at the courthouse, Nash had it locked and refused to turn over the key. Republicans countered a few nights later by hoisting a boy in through a window they pried open and having him open the door from the inside. The next morning, when Nash and his deputies, most if not all of whom had been present when Delos White was murdered, showed up, they were met by armed Republicans and turned away.

A few nights later, with Ward sick in bed after another flare-up of tuberculosis, James Hadnot called together a group of trusted associates and demanded that the courthouse be taken by force. The plot, which was supposed to remain secret, would be launched a few days later, on April 1.

But Hadnot could not help bragging about the coming battle, and word got back to William Ward. Forcing himself from his sickbed, Ward sent word out for his militia to come to the courthouse and guard against Hadnot's planned coup. When

Hadnot's forces showed up, they saw they were outnumbered and were forced to retreat.

After the Republicans took over the courthouse, they discovered some vital records were missing. On the assumption that the most likely place to find them was at the home of one of the two Democratic lawyers who had been sent to petition Governor Kellogg, they sent out black "deputies"—Ward had simply re-formed his militia and changed the name—to retrieve what had been taken. At one of the homes, that of William Rutland, the deputies terrorized the lawyer and his servants—he had sent his wife and children away to be sure they were safe—turning the house upside down and even breaking open a small casket that held the embalmed remains of the couple's dead two-year-old daughter.

Radical Democrats, who had felt beatings, whippings, and intimidation of freedmen were fully justified, now screamed about the barbarity of Radical Republican "usurpers." "The negroes of Colfax," reported the *Louisiana Democrat*, "proverbially a bad and turbulent set, lead [*sic*] by a few bad, very bad men, have taken entire and forcible possession of the Court House and Archives of the Parish of Grant, and driven off violently every decent white man, and have turned the town into an entrenched military camp . . . Thus far they have perpetrated many base and inhuman outrages . . . A large armed crowd went to the house of Judge Rutland, who had been previously driven away, searched and ransacked the house, destroyed the furniture, and broke open a coffin containing the remains of a child of the Judge's and threw its dead body into the road!"

Republican newspapers took a different view. "At all events," reported the *New Orleans Republican*, "there appears to have been nothing like a mob at Colfax at all, nor anything in the proceedings to warrant the assertion that the Republican officials did anything more than their duty required them to do in the premises. They found their places usurped by unauthorized persons, and took the obvious course to assert their rights."

With groups of armed men a regular sight on Grant Parish roads, neither side took much comfort in the newspaper reports. Many men sent their families away and barricaded themselves in their homes. Rutland fled, and James Hadnot, William Cruikshank, another prominent local landowner with a reputation for violence, and C. C. Nash began to think in terms of war.

In a final effort to avoid a bloody conflict, both sides agreed to meet and try to negotiate a settlement. After exchanging notes through an intermediary, they met in a field on April 5 and talks were actually showing promise, when the same black deputy who had led the raid on William Rutland's house rode up to say that Jesse McKinney was dead. Jesse McKinney was a black farmer who had helped defend the Colfax courthouse when James Hadnot's party had arrived on April 1. A group of armed whites had ridden up as he was building a fence around

Democratic political cartoon "Murder of Louisiana Sacrificed on the Altar of Radicalism."

his yard, and then one of them had shot him through the head while his wife and young son looked on in horror.

The deputy who had brought the news leveled his pistol at one of the white men and accused him and the others of knowing that black men were to be murdered while they engaged in phony peace talks. The deputy was persuaded to holster his weapon without firing, but both sides rode off without talking further. There would be no more negotiations.

Hours later, the armed band of whites that had gunned down Jesse McKinney headed for Colfax. But this time, Ward's men were ready for them. Twenty-five of them, all deputies, set themselves in a field outside of town to intercept the invaders. As soon as the unsuspecting white men were in range, the deputies opened fire. The white men returned fire but, shocked to be dodging bullets themselves, quickly retreated. The next day, a different group of armed white men approached Colfax, but they were beaten back as well.

The deputies reveled in their victories over men who had owned them just a few years before, but most of the other freedmen, lacking weapons or training, were terrified that they would be easy prey. They poured into Colfax by the dozens, hoping for protection. By April 7, the Monday before Easter, almost four hundred had sought shelter from the white mobs. Those who lived near James Hadnot were especially fearful, as Hadnot had made little secret of his intention to kill any black person who crossed him.

But the hope of sanctuary was false. Few of the black men

were armed and most of those who were carried old, barely functioning shotguns, not the sort of weapon to repel a serious attack. Ward would have given anything to have the Enfields back, but those had long since been returned to New Orleans. Most of the white men in the area owned modern rifles and pistols, and Hadnot had even persuaded the captain of a riverboat to remove his four-pound cannon—generally used to discourage pirates—for use against the black defenders in Colfax.

Hadnot and some others had also sent out a call for reinforcements, word that had reached as far away as Texas. As the numbers of white supremacists began to grow, it became clear that the Colfax defenders would have no chance if it came down to serious fighting. Ward sent a message to an African-American minister in Rapides Parish, but the minister was not going to send his parishioners to Colfax to fight against a mass of angry Klansmen.

On Wednesday, April 9, Ward realized that only federal troops could save them from defeat, the loss of the parish, and possibly death, so he and some others boarded a steamboat to appeal personally to Governor Kellogg and the army commandant in New Orleans. To those who remained, Ward promised aid if they could just hold on for a few days.

It would not be enough.

As Easter Sunday neared, James Hadnot and Christopher Columbus Nash prepared a force to invade Colfax and take back what they believed God and United States law meant to be theirs.

11

RECONSTRUCTION ASCENDANT—
BLANCHE K. BRUCE

LOOKING ONLY AT GRANT Parish, it would be tempting to con-
clude that those who insisted that Reconstruction was a
disaster were correct. And for a century, that was what most
historians—and most Americans—were convinced was true.

Reconstruction was a radical creation by Radical
Republicans, many insisted, a stain on the democratic process.
Articles, cartoons, and even a classic motion picture, *The Birth
of a Nation*, put forth images of lazy, brutish, illiterate black
men manipulated by corrupt, greedy carpetbaggers or "scalawags"—turncoat Southerners. Evil Northern whites and
savage, childlike blacks made a mockery of government. They
drove the South into chaos while "proper" white society was
forced to stand by helplessly, prohibited by Yankee soldiers
from preventing their own destruction. Southern women were
often prominently featured in these cartoons as threatened or
defiled victims—that black women had been regularly, system-
atically, and legally abused during American slavery's two
centuries was conveniently forgotten. Thaddeus Stevens in

particular was denounced as a tyrant entirely lacking feeling or human decency.

Finally, as this tale went, Redeemers, who were described as heroic, right-thinking white Southerners, rose up against these injustices and returned democracy, the Constitution, and good government to the Southern states. Black people, although free, were returned to the obedient status they deserved, allowed to thrive in those simple tasks for which they were suited. Andrew Johnson fared well in this legend, portrayed as a moderate and fair-minded man whose plans to continue the policies of Abraham Lincoln were frustrated by Stevens and the other fire-breathing Radicals.

A particularly dreadful 1942 film, *Tennessee Johnson*, had Van Heflin playing a noble Andrew Johnson, and a sneering Lionel Barrymore oiling his way through as Thaddeus Stevens. A Hollywood movie is just that, of course, but the portrayals of Johnson and Stevens were widely accepted as essentially accurate.

Nowhere was this view of Reconstruction and African-Americans painted more persuasively than in an article in the January 1901 edition of the *Atlantic Monthly*. The author was one of the nation's leading historians. He accused Radical Republicans of using "their restored power [to bring] absolute shipwreck upon the President's [Johnson's] plans." He added:

An extraordinary and very perilous state of affairs
had been created in the South by the sudden and

absolute emancipation of the negroes, and it was not strange that the southern legislatures should deem it necessary to take extraordinary steps to guard against the manifest and pressing dangers which it entailed. Here was a vast laboring, landless, homeless class, once slaves, now free; unpracticed in liberty, unschooled in self-control; never sobered by the discipline of self-support, never established in any habit of prudence; excited by a freedom they did not understand, exalted by false hopes; bewildered and without leaders, and yet insolent and aggressive; sick of work, covetous of pleasure, a host of dusky children untimely put out of school.

The article went on to denounce the Freedmen's Bureau and defend Black Codes, which reestablished slavery in all but name.

The author of this piece was living at the time in New Jersey, a respected faculty member of one of America's most famous universities. The following year, he would become its president. And ten years after that, he would be elected president of the United States. The university was Princeton and the historian was Woodrow Wilson.

But the picture painted in bad movies and by racist presidents has changed. Thanks to historians such as Eric Foner and John Hope Franklin, Reconstruction is now generally thought of as a noble experiment, flawed and uneven to be sure, but one that achieved some very real gains. If the program had been allowed to progress, supported in Washington and by white people in the North, the old Confederacy might have been permanently transformed, just as Thaddeus Stevens had predicted.

One major falsehood that has been set aside is that the Reconstruction governments were dominated by illiterate, gullible black men who were little more than stooges for carpetbaggers. Although more than two thousand African-Americans served in government positions during Reconstruction, most were in lower-level state or local positions, particularly as postmasters and justices of the peace, and almost never had any real control over state governments. Almost all political power during Reconstruction remained in white hands, and the vast majority of these whites had been born in the South, not the North.

Many, many Southern whites had opposed secession— quite a few, like William Phillips, had fought on the Confederate side—and they found homes in government after the war. And although Redeemers may have called them scalawags, many were simply trying to repair their devastated home states, and if the price was accepting freedmen as citizens (although not necessarily equals), they were willing to pay it.

While freedmen were free to elect a member of their own race regardless of qualifications, they often chose to vote instead for moderate whites. Most evidence indicates that African-American voters were not gullible followers at all, but rather took their responsibilities quite seriously. That many black voters could not read and write is true—as it was also true for many white voters—but most freedmen seemed to have made an effort to learn about the candidates and their positions before casting their ballots. In addition, illiteracy dropped sharply as schools were set up, and both children and adults were introduced to written language for the first time.

But certainly the most important of the new African-American officeholders were also the most prominent. The first in national office was Hiram R. Revels of Mississippi, who became America's first black senator in February 1870. Revels, who left the Senate one year later to become president of the newly established Alcorn University, was later referred to, probably by abolitionist Wendell Phillips, as "the Fifteenth Amendment in flesh and blood." Later that year, Joseph H. Rainey of South Carolina entered the House of Representatives.

During Reconstruction, only sixteen African-Americans served in Congress: one, P. B. S. Pinchback, served briefly as governor, in Louisiana; six served as lieutenant governors; two as state treasurers; four as superintendents of education; and eight in the largely ceremonial position of secretary of state. But these few might have been the seeds of far greater progress if not for the unwillingness of white America to fertilize the ground in which they had been planted.

To give a sense of the sort of person who might have led

such a flowering, one need only to look at the remarkable career of the second African-American elected to the Senate, also from Mississippi, and the only one to serve a full term.

Blanche Kelso Bruce was born in a slave cabin near Farmville, the county seat of Prince Edward County, Virginia, on March 1, 1841, the youngest of eleven children. Each of them, according to reports, was fathered by one of the two men who owned his mother, Polly. Newspapers after Bruce's death, however, said he was born to "slave parents," to avoid sullying the reputation of the white owners.

But his father, Polly's second owner, was a "kind and considerate man," according to Bruce's brother Henry, who gave his slaves "plenty of good, wholesome food." The family traveled a good deal, Polly either working in the house or hired out as a cook. At age four or five, Blanche became a playmate of his master's son and sat in when the white boy was taught to read and write. When Blanche was eight, his family was rented out to a plantation owner in Mississippi. For the first time in his life, Blanche experienced the backbreaking dawn-to-dusk toil of picking cotton under an overseer who made frequent use of his whip. Henry Bruce remembered "much rejoicing" when their master left Mississippi to move to Missouri.

Until he was twenty-one, Bruce either helped raise tobacco on his master's farm or was hired out to a local tobacco manufacturer. Henry later said that he and his brother were fed and clothed well, and that the factory owner allowed them to

Senator Blanche Kelso Bruce.

continue their education. The factory owner even gave them each an acre of land to grow and sell tobacco on their own.

But slavery, no matter how generously wrapped, is not freedom. As the nation descended further into the hatred that would soon erupt into war, Henry and Blanche eavesdropped on conversations and read newspapers when they could. When the fighting began and Bruce's owner headed south to join the Confederate army, Blanche had his chance. "After the firing on Fort Sumter and the opening of the war of the rebellion, I concluded that I would emancipate myself. So I worked my way to Kansas, and became a free man before the emancipation proclamation was issued by President Lincoln."

With no money, he worked at a variety of odd jobs to support himself. Then, in 1863, he opened a small school in a black town to teach local children to read and write. Quantrill's Raiders, a feared band of Confederate guerrillas, raided the town and burned much of it to the ground, including Bruce's school. Bruce escaped "by a miracle" and hid near the riverbank until the raiders had gone. He moved to Hannibal, Missouri, where ten years earlier, a local boy named Sam Clemens had left to seek his fortune east and would become known as Mark Twain. Blanche Bruce started a second school in Hannibal but, after the war ended, decided he wanted to become a minister. He enrolled at Oberlin College and received the only formal education he would ever have.

But once again with no money, he was forced to leave and took a job as a porter on a riverboat. There he read of a black man in Louisiana named P. B. S. Pinchback who was rising in state politics, and Blanche Bruce decided to give politics a try himself. He made a number of stops on his way south, but ended up in Mississippi, where he had picked cotton as a boy. He had seventy-five cents in his pocket.

His timing was perfect. Andrew Johnson's white supremacist governor had been removed, the Black Codes thrown out with him, and Mississippi's new Northern-born governor was looking for talented black men to put in government posts. When he met the soft-spoken, likable, obviously educated twenty-seven-year-old Blanche Bruce, he immediately gave him a job—supervisor of elections in Tallahatchie County.

Soon afterward, Bruce moved to Bolivar County and thrived. He was elected twice as county sheriff—with a good deal of white support—and he also went into business. His first purchase was 640 acres of prime cotton-growing land, where he started his own plantation—with well-paid workers. As the plantation became increasingly profitable, Bruce bought more land until, in 1874, he had become a wealthy man.

In those days, United States senators were not yet elected by popular vote but rather by a vote in a state's legislature. Bruce had visited the Senate gallery on a trip to Washington, DC, in 1872, and from then on made no secret of his desire to one day be a member of that chamber, where only one other man of his race had ever sat.

When the Mississippi legislature met for its 1874 session, both houses with solid Republican majorities, Bruce had his chance. He had realized that even though they did not control either house, Democrats could make his appointment difficult, so he had made it a point to do favors for many of the state's most important Democratic politicians. As a result, when Republicans pushed for his election, Democrats did not oppose it. On March 5, 1875, Blanche Kelso Bruce became the first African-American sworn in for a full term in the United States Senate. There would not be another for almost one hundred years.

But none of Bruce's term could be spent at home. It became clear that if he so much as set foot again in Mississippi, Redeemer groups intended to have him murdered. But even as an exile, he could make his voice heard—and he did. His first speech on the floor was to urge the Senate to seat P. B. S. Pinchback of Louisiana rather than the Fusion candidate who had arrived claiming the same seat. Pinchback's claim was clearly valid, but the Senate refused to seat him. Instead, they kept the seat vacant until 1876, when a Democrat, James B. Eustis, was accepted.

The 1876 elections in Mississippi were marked with rampant fraud and widespread intimidation of black voters by Redeemer groups. It was in the wake of that election that Senator Bruce made his most important speech. After denouncing "the corrupt and violent influences [that] were brought to bear upon the registrars of voters," and "the inspectors of election, prejudicially and unfairly thereby changing the number of votes cast" and the "threats and violence [that] were practiced directly upon the masses of voters," Bruce gave a ringing defense of his people.

"It will not accord with the laws of nature or history to brand colored people a race of cowards. On more than one historic field, beginning in 1776 . . . they have attested in blood their courage as well as a love of liberty. I have confidence, not only in this country and her institutions, but in the endurance, capacity, and destiny of my people. We will, as opportunity offers and ability serves, seek our places . . . Whatever our ultimate position in the composite civilization of the Republic and whatever varying fortunes attend our career, we will not forget our instincts for freedom nor our love of country."

Josephine Bruce.

During his term in the Senate, Bruce defended the rights of Native Americans; opposed the Chinese Exclusion Act, which absolutely banned Chinese labor immigration for ten years— the first restriction on a specific ethnic group in American history; and denounced the mistreatment of black cadets at West Point. When his term was done, he did not return to Mississippi but rather remained in Washington, working either in government or business. With his wife, Josephine Beall Willson, a highly educated woman, the daughter of a freeborn dentist in Cleveland, Ohio, Bruce became a fixture in Washington society.

Blanche Kelso Bruce died in 1898, a wealthy and respected man, with a rare and unique legacy.

EX-SENATOR BRUCE

EX-SENATOR REVELS

12

MASSACRE—JAMES HADNOT

AS EASTER SUNDAY DAWNED, the battle lines in Colfax were set.

C. C. Nash, who still considered himself sheriff of Grant Parish, had been amassing troops for most of the week. Officially, 165 men were in his party, but others had straggled in, so the number likely exceeded two hundred. They were extremely well armed, most with a long gun and pistol and some with three, even four, weapons. As a former army officer with two years of battle-hardened experience, Nash was the natural leader of the group. The others, even James Hadnot, deferred to his judgment. Nash deployed his men to ring the brick courthouse and had assigned a crew to wheel the four-pound cannon from the riverboat into position.

The defenders likely numbered about 150, although only about half of them were armed, again with only old, barely functioning weapons and almost no ammunition to put in them. At least an equal number of women and children were encamped just outside the courthouse as well. The men had spent the previous day and a half digging a trench for defense, but did not have time to make it deep enough to allow them to stand inside and fire. When completed, it was only about a foot deep, although mounds of dirt had been piled in front, allowing the defenders to lie prone without exposing anything but their faces.

Nash decided to give the freedmen a chance to surrender, and sent an emissary to request a meeting. The defenders agreed.

The two parties approached one another at the courthouse perimeter under a flag of truce. "We want that courthouse," Nash said.

But the freedmen remembered Jesse McKinney, to say nothing of the threats from Hadnot and others to murder any black man who defended the courthouse. They refused and said they would remain until troops came to protect them. What they did not know was that Governor Kellogg had been told the situation could be managed by those present and had decided against sending troops upriver.

Nash replied, "Then go in there and say to your people that I advise them to get out of there. I give you thirty minutes to remove your women and children."

The women and children were evacuated while Nash and his men waited. But even after only black men were left in and around the courthouse, Nash did not immediately attack. A charge was out of the question. The freedmen's shotguns could do little damage at a distance but could inflict serious wounds at close range. And his men were not soldiers, willing to accept a certain number of dead and wounded in order to take their objective. In fact, many of the men Nash and Hadnot had recruited had only been willing to join up after being assured they would not be put at risk.

The cannon was an impressive weapon, but was too far away to reach the trenches, let alone the brick courthouse. A couple rounds had been fired and succeeded only in kicking up large amounts of dirt. As a result, for about two hours, the two sides were at a standoff.

The turning point came when one of Nash's men found a spot to move the cannon where it would be sheltered from fire but still close enough to reach the trenches. After the first shot from that new position, one of the defenders in the trench was killed and others wounded. Realizing that their first line of defense was now useless, the freedmen in the trenches retreated to the safety of the courthouse.

But in the stampede to take refuge, the freedmen could not all get through the narrow doorway. When those who could not enter tried to run, the whites charged up the hill, most on foot, some on horseback. They shot down every escaping black man they could. Any who threw down their weapons and attempted to surrender were shot as well. Some black men begged for mercy but were murdered where they stood.

Those who made it inside the courthouse met a similar fate. Although the building was brick, the roof was wood shingle. As reported later by army officers who visited the scene, "A colored man named Isaiah Atkins informed us that Mr. Nash had forced a colored man called Pink to come to this end of the building [where there were no windows] and hold a pine torch to the edge of the roof until it caught fire."

As the fire spread along the roof, the burning shingles dropped into the building and soon the papers and wood inside were ablaze as well. Staying inside meant burning to death, so the freedmen had no choice but to pour out the door. Nash's men were waiting for them. They were ordered to throw down their weapons to surrender. The freedmen complied. But Nash was not there to take prisoners.

"When forced by the fire to leave the courthouse [the colored men] were shot down without mercy. Under the warehouse, between the courthouse and the river, were the dead bodies of six colored men who had evidently crept under for concealment, and were there shot like dogs. Many were shot in the back of the head and neck; one man still lay with his hands clasped in supplication; the face of another was completely flattened by blows from a gun, the broken stock of a double-barreled shotgun being on the ground near him; another had been cut across the stomach with a knife after being shot; and almost all had from three to a dozen wounds."

But black men were not the only fatalities. Three white men, including James Hadnot, were killed by gunfire. When questioned afterward, C. C. Nash had a ready account. As the army inspector recounted, "Mr. Nash stated that after the colored men got into the courthouse, they displayed a white flag, that [Messrs]. Hadnot and Harris went to see what was wanted, and on approaching the building were shot."

This statement was totally false. Not only was James Hadnot not killed by black men as he approached the courthouse under a flag of truce, he was almost certainly not killed by black men at all. The evidence is overwhelming that Hadnot was a victim of friendly fire, shot accidently by one of his own men.

When the whites charged up the hill, they did so from the semicircle in which they had taken positions. They were so aroused at the coming slaughter that they began to fire wildly, threatening their own men. James Hadnot jumped out and yelled for them to stop, that they were shooting at one another, when he was struck above the hip with a bullet that passed through his body and exited the other side. It would have been almost impossible for him to have been wounded in such a fashion while marching up the hill, holding a flag of truce. Another man received a similar fatal wound, while a few other whites were wounded and recovered. "Mr. Hadnot was shot through the stomach from side to side, and Mr. Harris in the back under both shoulders," the army officers confirmed.

When the main body of the defenders had been disposed of, the white men, again both on foot and horseback, began to search the surrounding areas and woods nearby. Most black men were slaughterd, but some were taken prisoner. There were prisoners from the courthouse as well, thirty-four in all.

As the army officers reported later, "It is asserted by the colored people that after the fight, thirty-four prisoners . . . were taken to the river bank, two by two, executed and buried in the river. We caused to be buried in the ditch near the ruins of the courthouse, the remains of fifty-four colored men, three of whom were so badly burned as to be unrecognizable. There were inside the courthouse the charred bones of one other, and five bodies we gave to their friends for interment elsewhere." When the column of prisoners was being marched off to be shot, one of them, Levi Nelson, whose life would be spared by being the second man shot with one bullet, heard another of the freedmen begging for his life. One of the white men replied, "I didn't come four hundred miles to kill niggers for nothing." The freedman who had begged for his life, like the other prisoners, was shot down.

The actual number of dead will never be known. Estimates ranged from sixty-five to more than four hundred. Although only about eighty bodies were accounted for, it is almost certain that many more were never found. The number most often given is 105, which matches a statement from a riverboat captain who landed at Colfax three days later and said, "It was reported to me that about 100 negroes had been killed and many wounded."

But of almost equal horror to the killings themselves was the joy of the white invaders in the aftermath of the massacre. A newspaper account a few days later gave a sense. "Mr. R. G. Hill, of Marshal [sic], Texas, a passenger on the Southwestern, furnished the *Times* with a written account of the affair, from which we make brief extracts: 'On arriving at Colfax we found about a hundred armed men on the bank, and most of the passengers, myself among the number, went ashore to view the battleground, for our young friend who came aboard at the wood pile informed us that if we wanted to see dead niggers, here was a chance, for there were a hundred or so scattered over the village and the adjacent fields, and he kindly offered to guide us to the scene of action. Almost as soon as we got to the top of the landing, sure enough, we began to stumble on them, most of them lying on their faces, and, as I could see, by the dim light of the lanterns, riddled with bullets.'"

13

THE WHEELS OF JUSTICE—
J. R. BECKWITH

NO MATTER HOW HORRIBLE the events at Colfax, obtaining justice for the victims was going to be extremely difficult. Grant Parish was in a remote area, with no permanent army presence, and white supremacists were now in charge. In fact, C. C. Nash, who had both murdered Delos White and led the force that massacred perhaps a hundred black men, was now back in place as sheriff. Freedmen, who had already gained a great deal of experience with unpunished murder, were all too aware that they would likely be killed themselves if they even hinted they might testify against the mob. To make finding, arresting, and punishing the killers even more of a challenge, most whites in Louisiana either secretly supported Nash's invaders or openly applauded them.

It would, then, take a man of exceptional commitment and courage, someone whose belief in equal justice for all was more important than public acceptance or even career advancement, to successfully pursue these killers.

It turned out that just such man was in New Orleans, occupying the very position from which prosecution of Nash and the rest of the Redeemer band must come.

James Roswell Beckwith was born in Cazenovia, in central New York State, about twenty miles southeast of Syracuse. The Cazenovia of Beckwith's boyhood was known for two things—farming and abolition. Antislavery ran deep in central New York, and fugitive slaves could always find many local people to either shelter them or pass them along to the next stop on the Underground Railroad. When Beckwith was seventeen, a huge rally against the Fugitive Slave Law was held in Cazenovia, in which Frederick Douglass was one of the speakers.

Beckwith's father was a successful farmer, but Beckwith himself felt a calling in the law. He moved to New York City to learn the profession, and after being admitted to the New York bar—which meant he was licensed to practice law in the state—he headed to Michigan, where he found a job as a district attorney. There he met and married Sarah Catherine Watrous, a cultured, educated woman who shared his views of slavery. She would become well known for her novel *The Winthrops*, a family saga that was published under the name Mrs. J. R. Beckwith in 1864.

For reasons that are not totally clear, the Beckwiths moved to New Orleans in 1860. While, as a thriving port, the city offered many opportunities to a young lawyer, there were other cities of that description that had neither slavery nor the oppressive heat and frequent epidemics of yellow fever and cholera that plagued New Orleans. When war broke out and Louisiana seceded, James and Catherine left the city, but returned in 1862 when New Orleans was captured by Union troops.

By the time the Civil War ended, J. R. Beckwith had a thriving law practice. But under the white supremacist, Andrew Johnson Reconstruction government, New Orleans was the scene of numerous incidents in which freedmen were beaten, tortured, and murdered. Soon after Johnson's allies were kicked out and Republicans took over, Beckwith was asked to become United States attorney for the region. A United States attorney is the federal government's equivalent of a district attorney, except he or she prosecutes only those offenders accused of federal crimes.

The offer was not entirely flattering. The previous occupant of the position had been found dead on the floor of his office, his throat cut. But Beckwith had witnessed too much injustice to refuse. Once in the office, he quickly established a reputation for honesty, dedication, and a total commitment to enforce the law without favoritism. To prosecute the Colfax case, he would need all of those qualities and more.

Almost immediately, Redeemers attacked on two fronts. With no federal authority in Grant Parish and C. C. Nash the sheriff, anyone who might be a witness was either terrified into silence or murdered. Outside of Grant Parish, Democratic newspapers began a campaign to portray the events as having been caused by the freedmen, who bore all responsibility for starting the "riot."

Typical is an editorial in the *Louisiana Democrat* on April 23, 1873. The freedmen, according to the article, had behaved like beasts.

> **Several times, after their evening drill, they would advance to the bank of the river and would salute the whites on this side with all sorts of obscene and savage threats, and telling them more than a dozen times that they (the negroes) were fixing for them and intended to kill the last of the men and children and violate their wives! In fact every threat, every curse that could be heaped on the white man were belched at them by these barbarians and inhuman negroes.**

So, the newspaper concluded, the whites had no choice but to act with honor.

> **The hour came that these white men had to act, had to defend their lives, their property, their wives, their children, and they did it in the best way they could, and the result has gone into history. The whites of Grant Parish were in the right, from first to last, and had exhausted every inch of patience and endurance in behalf of peace and quiet; and come what will, prosecutions and persecutions by the powers that be, a just and honorable world will hold them blameless and perfectly justifiable.**

Democratic newspapers also insisted that James Hadnot was gunned down without warning as he approached the courthouse under a flag of truce. Even worse, they claimed Hadnot had gone unarmed because the freedmen inside had asked to talk before surrendering. This was the version that C. C. Nash had given to the federal marshals, which they immediately knew was a lie, given the location of Hadnot's wound.

Nash proved himself an excellent diplomat when he needed to be. When an army unit of 150 men finally reached Colfax eight days after the slaughter, they were warmly greeted by Sheriff Nash, who assured them that peace had been restored and offered any assistance they might need. While it was obvious that many black men had died—more than a dozen bodies had not been buried, including that of Jesse McKinney, the farmer who had been murdered days before the massacre—Nash was ready with his tale of white self-defense.

Despite this blizzard of propaganda, J. R. Beckwith pushed forward, but there were serious legal issues as well. While the Constitution granted many powers to the federal government, many other powers had been reserved for the states. In fact, the Tenth Amendment, the last of the original Bill of Rights, stated, "The powers not delegated to the United States by the Constitution, nor prohibited by it to the States, are reserved to the States respectively, or to the people." One of the powers left to the states was to prosecute "ordinary crimes," such as theft, arson, embezzlement . . . and murder. The only way for Beckwith to pursue the killers, then, was to find a *federal* crime they had committed. For that, he looked to the Enforcement Acts that had been put in place to protect the guarantees of the Fourteenth and Fifteenth Amendments.

One of the few legal weapons Beckwith had available was a grand jury whose members were almost all Republican, with many African-Americans on the panel. In the weeks after the massacre, Beckwith prepared a list of charges, accusing C. C. Nash and ninety-seven other men with violating the civil rights of two of the victims, Alexander Tillman, who had been murdered, and Levi Nelson, who had survived.

As his legal basis, Beckwith cited Section 6 of the Enforcement Act of May 1870: "If two or more persons shall band or conspire together, or go in disguise upon the public highway, or upon the premises of another, with intent to violate any provision of this act, or to injure, oppress, threaten, or intimidate any citizen with intent to prevent or hinder his free exercise and enjoyment of any right or privilege granted or secured to him by the Constitution or laws of the United States, or because of his having exercised the same, such person shall be held guilty of felony, and upon conviction shall be fined or imprisoned, or both, at the discretion of the court." This meant that each of the ninety-eight men could go to jail simply because they had violated the civil rights of the two named victims.

Although the indictments were not approved by the grand jury in New Orleans until June, Nash and his fellows knew that they were likely to be arrested and once in custody, might remain so for ten years or more. They began to scatter. Some went to stay with relatives nearby, while others traveled well out of range of where troops might search. Still others, like C. C. Nash himself, remained in Colfax, waiting to see if Beckwith would be able to summon the manpower necessary to come upriver and arrest him.

As Nash suspected, Beckwith was finding it difficult to find resources to enforce his indictment. Beckwith's biggest problem was not Nash but his own boss, United States Attorney General George H. Williams. Williams had been appointed in 1871 to replace Amos Akerman, who had begun many prosecutions of Klan members under the very Enforcement Act that Beckwith intended to use against the Colfax killers. But Williams had been much less aggressive in trying to bring Klan members to justice—in fact, many thought he had been appointed specifically to slow the pace of expensive and time-consuming Klan prosecutions.

What Beckwith needed to round up the ninety-eight accused—or at least as many of them as he could find—were troops on horseback. Infantry could do a decent job of protecting a fixed location, like a town, but were unable to search the surrounding countryside. Cavalry could. When Beckwith asked for cavalry, he reminded Williams that he had promised to "spare no pains or expense to cause the guilty parties to be arrested and punished."

But that apparently did not include either mounted troops or money. Williams had been under pressure in Washington to spend less money on prosecutions against white terrorists.

George Williams.

He suggested that instead of a mass roundup, Beckwith iden-
tify six to twelve leaders of the assault and limit prosecution to
them. While Beckwith was certainly disappointed, it made his
job much easier. To get convictions against ninety-eight defendants, each man on trial would need to be identified by
witnesses. Only a few witnesses were still alive and willing to
testify in open court, and identifying almost one hundred
men would likely be impossible. But everyone had seen C. C.
Nash; Bill Cruikshank; Johnnie Hadnot, Jim's nephew; and
some of the other leaders.

When the time came to begin making arrests, summer had stretched into fall. Beckwith was receiving regular death threats, which were obviously not to be taken lightly. But he had committed to bringing to justice the men who had murdered unarmed men at Colfax, and he stayed true to that goal. With no mounted federal troops available, Beckwith came up with another plan. Army infantry would be stationed in the area as backup, but the actual arrests would be made by handpicked members of the state militia—they had horses of their own. Beckwith made certain that many of the militiamen would be black. Still, no one was making it easy for him. When he asked the army to sell him thirty days' supplies for his mounted force on credit, he was turned down. Yet, Beckwith pushed on.

It was not until the end of October that militiamen—now under federal authority—boarded a boat to steam upriver. Beckwith, Governor Kellogg, and a few other officials funded the excursion themselves, but were able to put up only enough money for a ten-day mission. Much of the expense went to refurbish a riverboat, including installing a brig to hold the prisoners—if they were lucky enough to have any.

Most of those on Beckwith's list had been warned and so, as many of the killers had done earlier, went into hiding or scattered out of Grant Parish. One went to Texas. But some had stayed put. The militiamen caught seven of the indicted men, including Johnnie Hadnot and Bill Cruikshank. That left one man among the most-wanted who had remained in the area—Christopher Columbus Nash.

As soon as word of the arresting posse had reached Colfax, Nash went into hiding with friends. He had switched locations more than once in case word of his location leaked out. The posse was preparing to return to New Orleans with its seven prisoners when they learned of Nash's location. After rotting in a Yankee prison for two years, Nash swore he would not be taken alive. As the posse roared toward the house where Nash was hiding, guns drawn, Nash leapt on his horse and made a dash for the wide Red River. As he was splashing through, the posse reached the riverbank and opened fire. With bullets splashing around him, Nash reached the far bank and the thick woods he knew so well. There was no chance that the militiamen from New Orleans could track him through unfamiliar terrain. In later years, white men told of Nash turning toward his pursuers and waving his hat before disappearing into the trees.

Christopher Columbus Nash, the man who shot Delos White at point-blank range and was a leader of one of the worst mass murders in American history, would never come to trial or even be arrested. Instead, he would marry the daughter of a successful planter, become a success in business himself, and live as an exalted member of his community until he died in bed in 1922.

14

CIVIL RIGHTS ON TRIAL

THE TRIAL OF COLFAX defendants did not begin until the end of February 1874. Although J. R. Beckwith was disappointed with the small number of defendants—now nine—just getting the case to this point was near miraculous. He had received little or no help from Washington, the army, local newspapers, and most Louisiana whites, all the while being threatened with a horrible death almost daily.

But as the trial was set to begin, it seemed Beckwith's persistence just might have been worth it. For a lawyer, there are four vital aspects of a criminal trial—the quality of the case, the presiding judge, the makeup of the jury, and the skill of the opposing lawyers. Beckwith had the first two of these solidly in his corner, and a third—the jury—seemed more favorable than it might have been.

The quality of his case was excellent. More than half a dozen African-Americans who had either been involved in the incident or witnessed it had agreed to testify. There is no overstating the courage it took for black people to travel to New

LIBRARY
JOHNS HOPKINS UNIVERSITY,
GIVEN BY

HORRIBLE MASSACRE

IN GRANT PARISH, LOUISIANA.

TWO HUNDRED MEN KILLED.

DETAILS OF THE OCCURRENCE.

MEETING OF COLORED MEN IN NEW ORLEANS.

ADDRESS AND SPEECHES.

NEW ORLEANS:
PRINTED AT THE REPUBLICAN OFFICE, 94 CAMP STREET.
1873.

Pamphlet detailing the events at Colfax, with witness statements.

Orleans and accuse powerful white men of murder and then be forced to travel home where friends and relatives of those very same white men had vowed revenge. That one of the most prominent of these was C. C. Nash, still on the loose, made testifying all the more dangerous. Although Beckwith had finally been able to get a small army unit placed in Colfax, its presence was certainly temporary.

Beckwith could be pleased with the judge as well. William Woods was born in New Jersey and graduated at the top of his class at Yale. He began the Civil War a Democrat who opposed Lincoln but ended it as a Republican who believed in a strong Union and equal rights. In between, he had enlisted in the army and was eventually promoted to general in Ulysses Grant's army. After the war, Woods had bought a plantation in Alabama, where he raised cotton. William Woods was smart, tough, fearless, and committed to the rule of law. From the first moment of the trial, he made it clear that only the evidence mattered—and the evidence did not favor the accused.

No matter how solid a case or fair a judge, of course, a jury that favors one side or the other can change the outcome of a case. In dozens, perhaps hundreds, of prosecutions across the South after the war, obviously guilty white defendants had been set free by all-white juries. But jury members are chosen from voter rolls and in 1874, the voting rolls in Louisiana contained thousands of African-American names. While in jury selection, each side has a certain number of "preemptory challenges"— people they can dismiss without giving a reason—there were so

Judge William B. Woods.

many black men in the pool that some of them were certain to make it to the jury. Of course, a certain number of Democrats would be on the jury as well, but Beckwith could only hope that once in a closed room with the other jurors, they would be fair and vote with the evidence, and not with their race.

The one area with which Beckwith could not have been pleased was the opposing counsel. The defendants had chosen two local lawyers known for both their skill in the courtroom and their own white supremacist views. They would be certain to try every legal trick to get their clients acquitted. But, on the first two days, when Judge Woods denied all the defense motions—requests to change how the trial would be conducted—Beckwith had cause for cautious optimism.

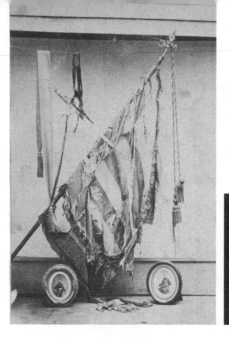

Battle-torn regimental flag of the 76th Ohio Infantry Regiment, during the Civil War, with photographs of Major General William Burnham Woods and his brother, Major General Charles Robert Woods, underneath.

The jury was, as expected, a mix of races and political views—five white Democrats, four white Republicans, and three black Republicans. In a criminal trial, however, a unanimous verdict is required to convict, so Beckwith needed to hope he could persuade five opponents to vote for justice. On Wednesday, February 25, 1874, he began the trial by asking the jury to do just that. He carefully laid out the particulars of the case, how he would prove by statements of men and women who were there that the defendants had murdered unarmed men—or at least murdered them after they had given up their weapons. He also reminded the jury that the men in the courthouse were there legally and had every right to defend both the building and themselves. It was the invaders who were acting in violation of the law.

Beyond the issue of the guilt or innocence of the defendants, Beckwith also needed to remind the jury that the Enforcement Act under which the accused were charged was the law of the land, enacted by Congress and signed by the president with the express purpose of protecting those whose rights might be violated and bringing to justice anyone who did so. According to the *New Orleans Republican*, "The attorney's recital was listened to attentively, as he deliberately related the leading horrors of the Colfax massacre."

Beckwith's first witness was white, a man who had been appointed as judge and seen his house burned to the ground by a mob after it became known that he intended to testify against the killers. He had sent his family away and barely escaped through a back door before his home was set ablaze. Willie Calhoun and William Ward also testified, but they could give only background since neither had been present for the killing.

But on Friday, February 27, Beckwith called to the witness stand someone who had been present, someone who by all rights should have been among the dead.

Levi Nelson made a powerful witness, not simply for what he said, but also for how he said it. A plain man, dressed in "Sunday best," Nelson spoke softly, and was sometimes halting, but never seemed unsure of what he was saying. His memory of the events was vivid and when he was cross-examined by one of the defense lawyers, he never wavered at all from his story.

He recounted what happened at the courthouse, how the black men had given up their arms under a flag of truce before they were slaughtered.

He then described what happened to him. "They kept me prisoner until midnight, then they took me and another man out to shoot us. One bullet struck me in my neck, stunning and dropping me. The other man was killed—they shot him five times. One man told somebody to shoot me again, saying that I was not dead. They did not shoot me again. I laid on the ground until morning, fearing to move, dead men all around me. I heard the men talking about killing niggers. I crawled off the field, not daring to get on my feet."

But it was when Beckwith asked Nelson whether he recognized any of defendants that the greatest drama occurred. As the *New Orleans Republican* reported, "A thrilling circumstance occurred last Friday, [Levi Nelson] who was wounded in the massacre, was on the stand, and when asked to name persons whom he saw in the fight, called out the names of several persons, among them the names of all but one of the prisoners at the bar. Mr. Beckwith told him to step down and point out the persons. The witness deliberately walked among them and confidently laid his hand on each. As he did so a thrill ran through the entire courtroom, for the act declared the men murderers: even attorneys for defense looked on gravely."

Beckwith called other African-American witnesses, each of whom risked his or her life by testifying.

One described how the killing started. "They first came up with their cannon. They halted about 50 yards from the courthouse: one of us tore off a shirt sleeve as a white flag, and shook it in the window; shelling did not cease then, but colored men were shot down as they left the courthouse, after the white flag was shown."

Beckwith called "the widow of one of the murdered men." She "related how she witnessed the bloody deed of the murder of her husband. She was standing in high weeds near the fatal spot where the victim was stood up to be executed. She heard him beg for his life, and she dared not lift a finger to save him. She saw the self-elected executioners aim their guns at his head and fire, and saw her partner drop dead almost at her feet. 'Clement Penn is the man, and there he sits!'" she said, pointing to one of the defendants.

Jesse McKinney's widow took the stand as well. She "clearly stated the manner of her husband's death. He was toiling near his home, when a band of marauders rode up and one of them deliberately shot him dead. 'The poor man was wet with the sweat of honest toil when he fell.' The corpse remained in the house several weeks, and was not interred until soldiers buried it."

When Beckwith had finished his parade of victims, it was the defense's turn. They made no attempt to deny that the killings had taken place but sought to portray the white men as simply protecting themselves and their families from a black mob set on pillage, rape, and murder. They brought a number of witnesses to the stand, even two who were black, but Beckwith was ready for them. Time and again, he punched holes in their stories. In particular, he demonstrated that if the defense witnesses were to be believed, James Hadnot and Sidney Harris, one of the other white men killed, could not have been shot from the courthouse.

By the time testimony was done and it was time for Judge Woods to charge the jury, only those most committed to the white cause could doubt that the defendants had done everything Beckwith claimed they had done—and likely more—and it was not in self-defense but simply for revenge and the love of killing.

The judge's charge to a jury, which takes place immediately before the jurors retire to a closed room to try to reach a verdict, can be crucial in determining how the jury will rule. In this case, how Judge Woods presented the Enforcement Act—why the defendants were charged under federal and not state law—might well determine how a juror would vote. There was a good deal of distrust of the federal government, some of which was shared by Republicans.

Judge Woods explained the law, which he called "a just and wholesome act," first. "This statute is the law of the land, and it is your duty and mine in a proper case to enforce it. Its purpose is the protection of all citizens of the United States of every class and condition, in the exercise and enjoyment of their lawful and constitutional rights. Its operation is equal. Its prohibitions are directed to all persons; its penalties fall upon all offenders against its provisions of every race, condition and party. No man who takes care not to invade the constitutional or lawful rights of another can be touched by it, and it protects alike the rights of all. It applies to all parts of our country, and its provisions extend to every State and Territory in the Union."

Woods then instructed the jurors "to dismiss entirely from your minds the idea that the prosecution is in the interest of any political party or faction." In other words, this was a crime, pure and simple, and they were not to consider the race of the victims but "render a just and true verdict according to the law and the evidence." Although Woods went on to note that the accused were innocent until proven guilty and that the burden of proof was on the prosecution to prove their guilt "beyond a reasonable doubt," few in the courtroom had any question that he believed Beckwith had done so.

Still, Judge Woods spoke for most of the day, carefully—and fairly—explaining every charge, every piece of law, and every possible verdict to the jury. That the case was of grave importance was clear to everyone in the packed courtroom, or as the judge put it, "On your verdict may depend the peace and order of the State."

It was near dusk when the judge finished and released the jury to begin its deliberations. Judge Woods and the court officers remained in their offices late into the night, not leaving until they felt certain that no verdict would be returned that day.

The weekend passed. Finally, at 8:00 p.m. Monday, the jury foreman sent a note to the judge. They could not reach a verdict on eight of the defendants. The ninth was found not guilty. With no unanimous verdict possible on the eight, a mistrial was declared. In such a case, the prosecution, in this case J. R. Beckwith, must decide if he wishes to once more go through the entire process and try the case again.

Most men would have realized that it would be impossible to get twelve men in New Orleans to vote guilty, but Beckwith was not willing to give up. He sent the accused back to jail and told Judge Woods he would try the case again.

15

IS JUSTICE LANGUAGE OR AN IDEA?—JOSEPH P. BRADLEY

JAMES BECKWITH WAS EXHAUSTED, both mentally and physically. He had worked almost nonstop for an entire year to bring the case against the Colfax murderers to court, all the while never knowing if one day he would suffer the same fate as Delos White. But it was typical of the man that for the second trial, he recruited even more witnesses and did all he could to make the case even stronger.

One way he did that was to make sure the jury pool held as many Republicans and African-Americans as possible. When a jury is chosen, it is not from every single person registered to vote, but rather from a "pool" of potential jurors selected from the voting rolls. Members of that pool get notices to report for possible jury duty and, after questioning by both sides, the appropriate number of jurors is chosen. The rest are free to return home.

In this case, the pool contained more than two hundred possible jurors, with a greater percentage of black and Republican members than existed in the voting rolls as a whole. The defense attorneys protested, as did the Democratic newspapers, but Judge Woods refused to order a change. In the end, only three of the jurors were black, but most of the white members had definite Republican sympathies.

The second trial began on May 18, 1874, but from the time the courtroom was called to order, it was clear that this one would be different. Although Supreme Court justices had loathed circuit riding since it was initiated in 1789, the requirement still existed—and would not formally end until 1911. And so, in addition to William Woods, the second trial would be heard by Associate Justice of the Supreme Court Joseph Philo Bradley. (Associate justice is the official title of every member of the court besides the chief justice.)

Joseph Bradley was in some ways perfect for the law. He was a careful man who rarely showed any feeling and was obsessed with order, detail, and punctuality. He was said to be "unconcerned with people, social life, or material rewards." Bradley, who called himself "cold and stoical," was set in his views, which were sometimes "narrow." He had few outside interests, and "his life was one of work, interrupted from time to time by his penchant for mathematics and chess."

Bradley had almost no close friends, but two he did have were from his college days at Rutgers College, in New Jersey. One of them, Cortlandt Parker—who would one day head the American Bar Association—said Bradley was "very little of a society man" and was "grave and sedate generally."

Justice Joseph P. Bradley.

But it would be difficult to describe Bradley better than he described himself. He recounted to Cortlandt Parker the routine he followed every day. "My habits are these: having sat up till 12 or thereabouts, I don't rise till 7. I then drink a glass of camomile water—dress, etc. and at 7 1/2 go into my study across the hall, and put on a pot of coffee (which is saved for me the day before) on the gas, and when hot—fill a large cup having cream and sugar in it—and drink it. Whilst drinking my coffee, an egg is boiling in the same gas jet—which I next dispose of. At 8, I am ready to go to work. At 9, I go down to family breakfast, and eat just one heaping tablespoon of mush (oatmeal, wheaten grits, or fine hominy) with cream and sugar, and return to my study. At 11 1/2 get into the coupe or carriage and go to the court which sits from 12 to 4. Return by 4 1/2 and lounge or take a walk, and dine at 6, generally light, on mutton, poultry, etc. I often take lunch at court about 2— of 6 broiled oysters, or a bowl of milk with a cracker or two. After dinner I return to my study, and generally work or read till midnight often topping it off with a glass of whiskey and water."

Bradley was from a poor family, one of twelve children, and his parents had little formal schooling. Unable to provide their son "even a common school education," they sent young Joseph to a winter school, one with a very short term. But there he excelled. Cortlandt Parker recalled Bradley's "education was of the simplest sort . . . but he was early renowned as a scholar. He was especially great in arithmetic . . . Devouring all books, he gave his special attention to the science of numbers, and with such success that at the age of fifteen, he was selected teacher of the winter school. Such precocity secured his local fame, and such stimulated his resolution to be a thorough educated man."

Eventually, he was sent to Rutgers College, at the time run by the Dutch Reformed Church. Bradley intended to study for the ministry. At the urging of Frederick Frelinghuysen, however, the second of Bradley's close friends—and a future United States senator—he switched to law and, after graduation, joined Frelinghuysen's legal firm. Bradley specialized in two fields in which lawyers were making a good deal of money—railroads and patents. Railroads had stretched from one end of America to the other, and thousands of miles of new track were being laid. Competition to use that track to haul freight and passengers was intense and so lawyers were always needed to settle disputes. It was also a time of great innovation, much of it involving railroads or industry. Lawyers were also needed to help inventors protect their creations and collect fees from anyone who wished to use them in their business.

Each of these specialties in what would come to be known as corporate law involved the long hours, ordered thinking, and extreme attention to detail for which Bradley had the perfect temperament. He soon became a successful, wealthy man, and his mastery of these new fields gained him a reputation in both New Jersey and Washington, where many railroad cases were tried. Under Ulysses Grant, the Republican Party had begun to move from being the Radical party of civil rights to the party of new and powerful American industrial corporations. And so, in 1869, when President Grant had an open seat on the Supreme Court to fill, he put forward Joseph P. Bradley, strictly on the basis of his record as a corporate lawyer, even though his nominee had no experience with constitutional law and had never sat as a judge.

In one way, Bradley was an excellent choice. There is little doubt that there were few men who could analyze the language of the law as finely as could he. He was logical, thorough, and had total attention to detail. But is the law only language or is it also an idea? Is the American Constitution only a series of articles, sections, and clauses, or is it something larger than that, an attempt for the first time in history to devise a government that would guarantee fundamental justice? Will there be times when simply breaking down the language to try to come to a definition defeats that goal of equal justice for all? The Constitution was flawed and has been added to—amended—for more than two centuries, but was it to better define language or to better define justice? And if Joseph Bradley was the perfect man to define the language, was he far less than the perfect man to define justice?

With the Colfax Massacre, Joseph Bradley, thrust into a pivotal crisis of American democracy, would provide the answer.

As an associate justice on the Supreme Court, Bradley outranked William Woods and would therefore conduct the trial for as long as he chose to be there, which could be as much or as little time as he pleased. According to the rules of the day, a justice riding circuit did not actually have to participate in a criminal trial, but Bradley, for reasons he never made plain, decided to do so with Colfax. With him present, however, the defense saw an opportunity they did not have in the first trial, which was to attack the prosecution on constitutional grounds, rather than just on the facts. In this case, that meant asking Bradley to declare that the federal court had no authority to try the case because the Enforcement Act was unconstitutional. Although throwing out the entire indictment was not the specific request, it would be difficult to try the case in a court not authorized to hear it. That of course would end the matter since a murder trial in state court was never going to take place.

The defense wasted little time in trying that very tactic. As soon as the jury was seated and before the opening statements were made, they asked Justice Bradley to end the trial because there was no federal case to be made. Although Bradley refused to end the trial, neither did he rule that the federal court had a right to try it. He would wait and make that ruling later, either during the trial or after the verdicts had been announced. The trial would proceed without anyone, except perhaps Justice Bradley, having any idea of whether or not everyone was wasting their time.

A few days later, that prospect became more likely. Suddenly and without warning, just as James Beckwith was questioning witnesses, Justice Bradley ruled that the defense could indeed present their arguments that the case should not be heard in federal court. And they could do it right then, interrupting the prosecution's case and in front of the jury.

Beckwith protested, Judge Woods seemed shocked, and the defense lawyers were thrilled. Before the Civil War, while Joseph Bradley was firm in his opposition to secession, he had expressed equal opposition to the abolition of slavery. He believed slaveholders should have received compensation if their slaves were freed by Union troops. He also spoke in favor of allowing Southern states to do what they pleased without federal interference, which meant letting Black Codes stand. In a letter to his daughter, Bradley called the Freedmen's Bureau "an engine of mischief, that teaches the Negroes to be discontented; gives them false notions and utterly incapacitates them from labor." Once on the Supreme Court, he had expressed great sympathy for Southern whites.

So, while James Beckwith viewed Bradley's presence as "a nightmare," the defense finally had their chance to get the case thrown out without relying on the testimony of witnesses even they knew were lying.

Their argument was simple. The rights of peaceable assembly and to keep and bear arms in the First and Second Amendment only protected citizens of the United States against action by a *state*, not "against aggressions by individuals." And so "the protection of these rights to individual citizens against violation by individual citizens is left to the local State Government alone." In other words, since no official state action was taken against the men murdered at Colfax, the case could only be tried in state court. The same was true of the Fourteenth Amendment—it only protected individual citizens against action by a state government, not other individuals. As such, the Enforcement Act of 1870 also could not be used to prosecute ordinary criminals, and any attempt to do so was unconstitutional.

Bradley praised the defense lawyer for the quality of his arguments, and "took the matter under advisement." He did not make a firm commitment to rule later, either before or after the verdicts had been handed down. He did, however, promise the defense lawyers that if any of their clients were found guilty, they could once again raise these same objections and ask for the guilty verdicts to be thrown out. After that pronouncement, Justice Bradley left the courtroom and, the next day, took a boat to Texas. He did not return, leaving the actual trial to Judge Woods.

Under this cloud, the trial proceeded. Beckwith called witness after witness to recount the horrors of Colfax and the defense called an almost equal number of witnesses to testify that, against every appearance to the contrary, the white invaders had acted in self-defense.

On June 9, after passionate closing arguments from prosecution and defense, the case went to the jury. At 7:30 the following evening, they sent the judge a message that they had reached a verdict. The prisoners were brought into the courtroom, followed by the jury members. At 8:30 p.m., the verdict was read.

Five of the defendants were acquitted.

But three were found guilty.

William Cruikshank, Johnnie Hadnot, and Bill Irwin, all of whom had been heavily involved with murdering prisoners, had been held accountable for their crimes.

Republicans were pleased that there had been at least some guilty verdicts, although disappointed only three of the original ninety-eight had been convicted. Democrats were furious.

The *New Orleans Bulletin* called the verdict "The Last Judicial Outrage" and ran the headline "Three White Men Defending Their Rights and Their Families Found Guilty." The newspaper made it a point to publish the names of the jurors, which, given how often those going against white supremacy had been beaten and murdered, was certainly not an innocent act.

But Democrats seemed to have forgotten for the moment that the case was not over. An item in the *New Orleans Republican* explained why. "Judge Woods informed counsel that he had telegraphed the verdict to Justice Bradley, as the latter had declared that in the event of a conviction he would consider and pass on a motion made by defense to erase certain portions of the indictment."

Two weeks later, that was precisely what Justice Bradley did. In a surprise, Bradley returned to New Orleans to deliver his opinion rather than submitting it by mail as everyone expected. As he walked into a packed courtroom on June 27, everyone, including Judge Woods, sat silently. At stake was not simply the fate of the Colfax defendants but the future of African-Americans in the South—whether they could live without fear and enjoy the very rights that the Constitution had promised them. Justice Bradley's opinion would prove to be one of the most important in United States history, one that in many ways would decide if the Constitution actually *was* what it *should be*. It was as if the law was on trial against justice.

For Justice Bradley, the choice was easy. In a long, extremely detailed opinion, he sided entirely with the defense and ruled that the federal government had no authority under the Constitution to prosecute the Colfax defendants. His reasoning was like the man himself—logical, carefully written, and thorough, but also cold, inward-looking, and narrow.

The constitutional question on which Bradley ruled was deciding when the United States government had authority to pass laws controlling the behavior of ordinary citizens, and when only states could do so. During Reconstruction, the federal government had taken on the responsibility of guaranteeing basic—and constitutional—rights when state governments could not be trusted to do it. In other words, private individuals had been compelled by federal law to adhere to the Bill of Rights. But did the Constitution, where the Tenth Amendment separated powers between the federal government and the states, allow the Congress and the president to do that?

To Bradley, the answer to that question was almost always no. There were exceptions, times when the federal government could control the behavior of private citizens—could prosecute "ordinary crimes"—but some very specific conditions had to be met. In defining those conditions, Justice Bradley changed the meaning and power of both the Fourteenth and Fifteenth Amendments. If his interpretation stood, black people in America could be returned to a condition that was slavery in all but name.

Bradley insisted that the only time the federal government could pass "positive laws" to protect individual rights was if that right did not exist before the Constitution defined it. The notion of "new rights" was as confusing to most lawyers as to everyone else, so to illustrate his point, Bradley gave some examples. One took such a narrow view of the Fifteenth Amendment that it would doom black voting rights for a century.

He wrote, "The Fifteenth Amendment confers no right to vote. That is the exclusive prerogative of the states. It does confer a right not to be excluded from voting by reason of race, color or previous condition of servitude, and this is all the right that Congress can enforce." In other words, if a black person was threatened, beaten, his house burned to the ground in order to terrorize him into not voting, and the state refused to prosecute the offenders, the federal government could do nothing—unless the black person could *prove* that the actions were motivated *only* by race. That to prove such a thing was almost impossible—unless the attacker publicly announced it—did not at all concern Justice Bradley. He had willingly communicated to any Redeemer that to avoid federal prosecution, he needed simply to keep his mouth shut before committing murder.

For J. R. Beckwith and the Colfax prosecution, Bradley's definition was fatal. He had not made any attempt to *prove* what he and everyone else thought was obvious—that the Colfax defendants had acted because of race. It would not have occurred to him that the execution of perhaps one hundred black Americans by a mob of white men would not be seen by everyone as a racially motivated act. But in being unaware of Bradley's new rules, Beckwith had broken them.

Bradley wrote that Beckwith's indictments did "not contain any allegation that the defendants committed the acts complained of with a design to deprive the injured persons of their rights on account of their race, color, or previous condition of servitude." And that, to Bradley, was "an essential ingredient in the crime to bring it within the cognizance of the United States authorities." Bradley admitted that "perhaps such a design may be inferred from the allegation that the persons injured were of the African race, and that the intent was to deprive them of the exercise and enjoyment of the rights enjoyed by white citizens." But since Beckwith hadn't mentioned it specifically, Bradley threw the charge out.

But Bradley was not finished. Not only had United States Attorney Beckwith overstepped his authority, so had the United States Congress. The Enforcement Acts provided for protections and penalties that only states could make into law. Once again, he used his narrow definition of the Fifteenth Amendment to demonstrate his point. (His definitions of the Fourteenth Amendment's "due process" and "equal protection" clauses were every bit as narrow.)

The fourth section of the Enforcement Act made it a crime "for any person, by force, bribery, threats, etc., to hinder or prevent, or to conspire with others to hinder or prevent, any citizen from performing any preparatory act requisite to qualify him to vote, or from voting, at any election." This was precisely the sort of protection Bradley had insisted the federal government had no authority to guarantee. "This section does not seem to be based on the Fifteenth Amendment," he wrote, "nor to relate to the specific right secured thereby. It extends far beyond the scope of the amendment."

In the end, the power of enforcement "does not authorize congress to pass laws for the punishment of ordinary crimes and offenses against persons of the colored race or any other race. That belongs to the state government alone."

So the case rested on whether the actions of the Colfax defendants were a violation of a constitutionally guaranteed right or an ordinary crime. And the former was restricted to actions by the defendants that were based explicitly on racial grounds. Lacking absolute proof that the Colfax defendants murdered the freedmen in Colfax only because of the color of their skin, federal authorities had no right to intervene in what was then simply a state matter.

The convictions, therefore, must be overturned.

Beckwith was stunned. He had spent a year of his life trying to gain some bit of justice for the victims. Black men and women had risked their lives to testify against the accused. The federal government was the only entity that prevented Redeemers from launching a reign of terror across the South. Most of all, while there was no shortage of evidence that the

Voter discrimination in 1874.

defendants wanted to "kill niggers," how could anyone ever prove that race hatred was their *only* motive?

Judge Woods was equally distressed. He announced "that while he regarded the opinion of Judge Bradley with appropriate deference, his opinion on the validity of the indictment had been carefully formed and was of long standing. He was, therefore, compelled to dissent from the views expressed by his learned brother."

That Judge Woods disagreed meant that the matter would not end in New Orleans. According to the rules, such a disagreement between sitting judges meant that the case would be finally decided only in the Supreme Court.

16

THE MOST IMPORTANT JUDGE IN THE NATION— MORRISON WAITE

JOSEPH BRADLEY WAS NOT the only appointment to the Supreme Court that Ulysses Grant would make. On May 8, 1873, Chief Justice Salmon P. Chase died. He had been ill for quite a while, paralyzed on his right side since 1870, but continued to do his job until his illness suddenly got worse and overcame him. If Roger Taney's departure was greeted with relief, Chase's was met with regret.

The *New York Times* said, "His devotion to lofty aims was proven at a time when such devotion was severely tested, and he never lacked—certainly never while engaged in active political life—the courage of his convictions . . . Whether we regard his services as a leader in a political movement for the restriction and ultimate extinction of slavery . . . or as head of the Supreme Court in the trying period succeeding the close of the war, we may be sure that his mark on the history of his times will for a long time be distinctly recognized."

Even adversaries recognized Chase's achievement. The *Brooklyn Daily Eagle*, one of the leading Democratic newspapers in America, and no fan of either President Lincoln or his appointees, said of Chase, "He was in important respects, the most distinguished and ablest man having to do with American affairs in modern times."

With such large shoes to fill, President Grant was immediately put under pressure to appoint a replacement of equal stature and reputation. Rumors began to circulate almost immediately, but the list of names passed about was large. Some thought Grant would nominate one of the other justices, others guessed he would ask a prominent lawyer to take the job, while still others insisted it would be a member of Congress.

But Grant refused to make a decision. May gave way to June, and then summer to fall, but still the president refused to name a successor. With every passing week, the nation became more impatient. Democrats accused Grant of not caring enough about the most important court in the nation, while Republicans declared that he was taking his time so he could choose the best, most honorable, most qualified man available.

But Ulysses Grant did not make his appointments based on honor and qualifications—he wanted people around him whom he knew and he could trust. That was why the Grant presidency became notorious for "cronyism"—making political appointments based on personal friendship. Many of Grant's cronies turned out to be corrupt, using government connections to increase their personal wealth or power.

Finally, in early November, Grant made his choice, and it was the ultimate crony, Senator Roscoe Conkling of New York. Conkling was one of the president's closest personal friends, and also perhaps the most powerful and feared politician in America. He was described as "about as well suited for the bench as for a monastery." The prospect of a man known as the "king of partisanship" becoming the leader of the body whose job it was to judge issues fairly was met with scorn. *Harper's Weekly* wrote, "The nomination of . . . Conkling [has been met] with universal amazement" and that he was "singularly unfitted to be a Judge." *The Nation* added, "Mr. Conkling is a lawyer only in name, and must make a poor Judge. He has passed his life in politics . . . Legal learning, he has not." The *Brooklyn Daily Eagle* said Conkling had a "fondness for controversy and affairs, rather than for judicial study."

There was little question that Conkling's immense power in the Senate had come from trading favors and making secret deals both with other members of Congress and with businessmen. But Conkling was also a fervent supporter of equal rights. When Blanche Bruce came to the Senate and was forced to endure taunts and even threats from his fellow senators, it was Conkling who provided him protection. So grateful was Bruce that he named his son Roscoe Conkling Bruce in the New York senator's honor.

Before submitting Conkling's name to the Senate, Grant wrote to him on November 8, 1873, to offer him the job. "When the Chief Justiceship became vacant, I immediately

An 1880 political cartoon showing Roscoe Conkling, "The Boss," trying to decide the man he will pick for president. He was sometimes said to be more powerful than the president.

looked with anxiety to some one whose appointment would be recognized as entirely fitting and acceptable to the country at large. My own preference went to you at once." This after waiting six months.

Roscoe Conkling was many things, but a fool was not one of them. Moving to the Supreme Court, even as chief justice, would diminish his vast power in government. He declined the appointment, a move described as "fortunate for the nation."

With Conkling unwilling to serve, Grant cast about for a replacement and, on December 1, he "stunned the nation" by nominating his attorney general, George H. Williams, the man who had done so little to support J. R. Beckwith's prosecution of the Colfax killers. Although some Republican newspapers fell into line and supported the nomination, most attacked a man widely considered a "legal mediocrity" and "a weak if not corrupt politician who would have doubtless been hopeless as Chief Justice."

Democratic newspapers were fierce in the criticism. The *Brooklyn Daily Eagle* described Williams as "knowing little of all law and less than that little of the law requisite for the Government cases." Ohio's *Columbus Statesman* added, "President Grant has again given a surprise to the country in the appointment of Attorney General Williams as Chief Justice of the United States. Mr. Williams was the most unfit man of any that were urged for the position. As a Senator he was weak, and when the President made him Attorney General surprise was manifested in every quarter."

But independent journals and a surprising number of Republican newspapers were highly critical as well. The *Evansville Courier* observed, "Judicial positions in the United States at the present time seem to be going begging, and legal talent and judicial ability is a lamentably scarce commodity . . . Williams is, without doubt, an obscure lawyer . . . recognizable only as one of the White House flunkeys, and is about to reap the reward of the faithful servant in that connection." The *Milwaukee News* added, "President Grant has a rare knack of drawing around him and pressing into the public service a class or people who never previously earned sufficient distinction in any walk of life to be lifted above the level of what might be called nobodies . . . Perhaps we ought to be thankful that the President did not bestow the place in gratitude on the savior of his late sick colt or the last donor of an acceptable gift." The *St. Louis Republican* was especially vicious. "Evidently the President has learned nothing and forgotten nothing, and proposes to continue as he has begun. With such a Cabinet, such Foreign Ministers and such a Chief Justice, he may confidently trust that history will lose sight of his own feebleness in the chronic imbecility of the large proportion of those individuals who adorn his administration."

While Republican senators could not be as openly harsh, they too thought Williams an extremely poor choice. They demonstrated their displeasure by doing nothing. Where Chief Justice Chase had been confirmed by the entire Senate the very day his nomination was sent to them by President Lincoln, this Senate refused to vote and instead sent the nomination to its judiciary committee for "consideration." And there it sat. Although the committee members eventually voted to send the nomination to the full Senate, public outcry forced them to reconsider. After a time, Williams, undoubtedly greatly embarrassed, officially asked the president to withdraw his name. He later wrote that he was "surprised, as was the President, at the opposition of some of the Republican Senators," although he claimed the reasons "were not those given in the newspapers."

Grant was once again forced to seek a suitable nominee, and he chose a man with an excellent reputation for intelligence and diplomatic skill, seventy-three-year-old Caleb Cushing. Cushing had recently been appointed to negotiate a treaty with Spain and was planning on leaving for Madrid in mid-January, when he was informed that he had been nominated as chief justice. Cushing had a long record of service, including as attorney general under President Franklin Pierce. Like Joseph Bradley, Cushing had spoken out against secession but had also opposed the abolition of slavery. Although he had not done so actively, Cushing was known to have opposed going to war to keep the Union together, and certainly not to free slaves. He also had the reputation as a man who would "place political opportunity before principle."

Like that of George Williams, Cushing's nomination on January 9 was a surprise to everyone, including the nominee who was "packing his trunks in order to be off by the first steamer for England, en route to Spain."

Unlike Williams, Cushing did not provoke strong opposition, nor did he generate much enthusiasm. But just when it appeared that President Grant had finally found a nominee that would be successfully confirmed, an "anonymous source" reported that in 1861, Cushing had sent a very friendly letter to Jefferson Davis, president of the Confederate States of America, accepting the split in the Union as "accomplished fact." Grant then found the letter itself and immediately withdrew Cushing's nomination.

Back to having no one suitable to name chief justice, Grant decided that his next nominee would have no trouble being confirmed. To achieve that, he resolved to choose someone no one in Washington had heard of. He found his man in Toledo, Ohio, a successful lawyer who had occasionally appeared at the fringes of politics—the one time he ran for office, he lost—but who had never tried a case before the Supreme Court, or in Washington at all.

His name was Morrison Remick Waite. Attorney General Williams, himself a reject, described the process by which Waite was selected. "Morrison R. Waite, of Ohio, was supposed to be sufficiently obscure to meet the requirements of the occasion. One can readily imagine the surprise of Mr. Waite when I telegraphed to know if he would accept the office of Chief Justice. He had never dreamed of such a thing . . . Judge Waite at the time of his appointment had never held a federal office, had never argued a case in the Supreme Court, and was comparatively unknown in Washington."

To those who had heard of him, Waite was unimpressive. Lincoln's secretary of the navy, Gideon Welles, remarked of Waite that "it is a wonder that Grant did not pick up some old acquaintance, who was a stage driver or bartender, for the place." *The Nation* added, "Mr. Waite stands in the front rank of second rank lawyers." The *Chicago Daily Tribune* summed things up: "Although his practice has been extensive, he is not

Chief Justice Morrison Waite.

credited with the possession of more than a comfortable competence. His confirmation is conceded."

As it was. Perhaps because Congress was now too fatigued to object, Waite was unanimously confirmed and took his seat on March 4, 1874.

Waite was not greeted warmly by his fellow justices. Not only had they been passed over for the seat Waite now held, but most of them regarded their new boss as an undeserving mediocrity. The only associate justice who extended Waite any courtesy was cold, unsociable Joseph Bradley, who invited the new chief justice and his wife to dinner their first night in the nation's capital.

17

CIVIL RIGHTS—
CHARLES SUMNER

ON MARCH 11, 1874, exactly one week after Morrison Waite was sworn in as chief justice, Massachusetts senator Charles Sumner died. Sumner had been one of the giants of Radical Reconstruction, Thaddeus Stevens's counterpart in the Senate. He left a long record fighting for equal rights—and in his case, *fighting* meant just that. In May 1856, after delivering a speech denouncing a South Carolina senator for forcing himself on female slaves, Sumner was nearly beaten to death with a cane on the floor of the Senate by South Carolina congressman Preston Brooks, the accused senator's cousin.

Sumner was absent from the Senate for almost three years, but when he returned, his zeal to end slavery and establish equal rights for black people was undiminished. After the war, he let no one and nothing decrease his determination to force the United States to become the nation it had promised to be—for all its people.

One of his main goals was for the United States to enact laws that guaranteed equal treatment in all aspects of daily

Preston Brooks beating Charles Sumner on the floor of the Senate. The caption is "Southern Chivalry."

life. On May 13, 1870, he introduced what he called a "supplementary" to the 1866 Civil Rights Act—the one "To Protect All Persons in the United States in Their Civil Rights and Liberties"—in which the federal government would specifically guarantee "equal rights in railroads, steamboats, public conveyances, hotels, licensed theaters, houses of public entertainment, common schools and institutions of learning authorized by law, church institutions, and cemetery associations incorporated by national or State authority; also in jury duties, national and state." The notion of enforced integration in schools and churches—in the North as well as the South—gave even most Republicans pause. Sumner got nowhere. A number of prominent Republicans, such as Lyman Trumbull from Illinois, who had introduced the 1866 bill, even took the position that both the Civil Rights Act of 1866 and the Fourteenth Amendment demanded only that facilities available to the races be equal. Freedom of association or, in the case of churches, free exercise of religion, would prevent the federal government from requiring that the races actually mix. "If the facilities for education are the same nobody has a right to complain," Trumbull asserted. Undeterred, Sumner reintroduced his supplementary the following year with the same lack of results.

Even as the Republican Party quite publicly began to drift away from the Radical vision, Sumner refused to abandon his proposal; he hung on to the church provision until December 1873. A willingness to settle for a less sweeping guarantee of equal access to public facilities might have gained him support, but Sumner refused to compromise. He pushed on, expecting that, in the end, the Senate would give in and "crown and complete the great work of Reconstruction."

But Sumner's influence had all but disappeared. Finally, as 1874 dawned, Sumner, ill and dispirited, was finally willing to accept less, but the time had passed even for that. Most Republicans did not intend to revisit a subject that had already lost them so many voters. Twice, Sumner attempted to have a watered-down bill approved by the Republican-dominated judiciary committee, and twice he failed.

As a result, when Charles Sumner died in March 1874, it was with his most treasured ambition, full equality under the law, unfulfilled. But then, in a bizarre twist, the bill that Sumner had tried so hard to get passed began to gain momentum. Benjamin Butler, Sumner's fellow senator from Massachusetts, was determined to enact some version of the supplement as a tribute to his fallen colleague. To everyone's amazement, most of all to Butler's, the tactic seemed to work. "Champions of equal rights seldom heard from before sprang up to defend the bill's constitutionality and its reasonableness." After a good deal of debate, the Senate passed the bill in May 1874, but then the House refused to follow along. The bill was set aside without being brought to a vote while the congressmen returned home to campaign for 1874 elections.

When Congress reconvened in December 1874 for its "lame-duck" session—that is, when many of those who lost their seats in the November elections still got to finish out their terms—the supplementary was still pending. But the just-completed elections had been a disaster for Republicans. When the new Congress was sworn in on March 4, 1875, the House of Representatives would shift from a 199 to 88 Republican majority to a 182 to 103 edge for the Democrats. Since only a third of the Senate had been up for reelection, Republicans would keep control, but a 54–19 majority would shrink to 47–28, and would surely shrink further in 1876. President Grant would also complete his second term in 1876, and a Democrat was favored to succeed to the presidency.

Butler renewed the fight. Despite reluctance among

Republicans and a Democratic filibuster that reduced senators to "whiling away the hours by tearing newspapers to shreds [as] stale cigar smoke choked the air, and members sprawled on the unswept carpet," Butler got the bill passed by both houses of Congress, although the schools and cemeteries provisions had to be dropped. Section 1 of the final bill read, "All persons within the jurisdiction of the United States shall be entitled to the full and equal enjoyment of the accommodations, advantages, facilities, and privileges of inns, public conveyances on land or water, theaters, and other places of public amusement; subject only to the conditions and limitations established by law, and applicable alike to citizens of every race and color, regardless of any previous condition of servitude." President Grant signed the bill into law on March 1, three days before the new Congress would take office. The preamble of the new law, "An act to protect all citizens in their civil and legal rights," proclaimed it "the duty of the government in its dealings with the people to mete out equal and exact justice to all, of whatever nativity, race, color, or persuasion, religious or political." For the first time, it seemed, the promise of Thomas Jefferson's famous passage in the Declaration of Independence asserting that "all men are created equal" would be kept. Jefferson, a slaveholder himself, almost certainly meant only white men.

For those freedoms guaranteed in Section 1 of the law, Section 2 listed penalties for those who would deny to any American fundamental rights of citizenship—up to $500 for each offense, payable to the victim; and, if convicted in criminal court, an additional fine for the offender of between $500 and $1,000 and up to one year in jail. Section 3 gave federal rather than state courts jurisdiction over suits arising from "offenses against, or violations of, this act." Section 4 guaranteed that no citizen could be disqualified for service as a juror in either federal or state court "on account of race, color or previous condition of servitude."

The wording, which very much matched much of that of the Fourteenth and Fifteenth Amendments, seemed to be a response—and a challenge—to Joseph Bradley's Colfax opinion. Congress could easily be seen as telling the judiciary that it was only they who had the power to make law.

Passage of the Civil Rights Act elicited passionate responses. Black Americans rejoiced and moved immediately to exercise their new freedoms. Hotel owners, theater managers, restaurateurs, tavern owners, and railroad agents were suddenly overwhelmed with requests for first-class rooms, choice theater seats, front tables, or a beer at the bar. Most whites, however, were equally determined to continue to exclude African-Americans from just those privileges. The notion of black mixing with white was sufficiently unpleasant that most of the white population either ignored the law or broke it, with almost total support of police, politicians, and the courts. Across the Potomac from the nation's capital, the owners of the two principal hotels in Alexandria, Virginia, elected to close rather than be forced to rent rooms to black

Speech in the House of Representatives by South Carolina congressman Robert B. Elliott, an African-American, in favor of the Civil Rights Act of 1875.

Americans. Both quickly reopened when the owners realized that refusing black guests would not actually land them in any legal difficulty. In Memphis, four African-Americans demanded to be seated in the dress circle at a local theater. When the management grudgingly acceded, most of the white patrons walked out. In Richmond, Virginia, African-Americans demanded service in restaurants, a tavern, and a barbershop, but in each case were refused.

The *New York Times*, which had praised passage of the Fourteenth Amendment in 1868 as "settling the matter of suffrage in the Southern States beyond the power of the rebels

A cartoon featuring an African-American telling Saint Peter that he can't object to keeping the heavenly gates open after the passage of the Civil Rights Act of 1875.

to change it, even if they had control of the government," denounced the law in an editorial. "It has put us back in the art of governing men more than two hundred years . . . startling proof how far and fast we are wandering from the principles of 1787, once so loudly extolled and so fondly cherished."

But the *Times* knew where to look for relief. "The Supreme Court, in instances such as this, is the last hope of all who attach any value to . . . the Constitution of the United States."

The *Chicago Daily Tribune* predicted the law would have little practical impact. "At present, its effect will be mainly political. It will be used on the one side to retain the hold of the Republican Party on the negroes of the South; on the other, to excite new opposition to the Republican party among the whites." The newspaper agreed that the constitutionality of the bill would be settled in the Supreme Court.

That test would begin just four weeks later when, on March 31, 1875, *United States v. Cruikshank* was heard by Morrison Waite's Supreme Court.

18

ONE HUNDRED YEARS OF FREEDOM—PHILADELPHIA AND THE WHITE LEAGUE

THE YEAR 1876 PROMISED to be very special in the United States of America. It would be one hundred years since thirteen colonies declared their independence from Great Britain with a document that declared, "We hold these truths to be self-evident, that all men are created equal, that they are endowed by their Creator with certain unalienable Rights, that among these are Life, Liberty and the pursuit of Happiness." (The fact that "pursuit of happiness" was a substitute for "property" because no one quite knew how to deal with slaves had been long forgotten.) To commemorate the signing of that document, a grand celebration was required, and where better than in Philadelphia, the city where both the Declaration of Independence and the Constitution were born?

Planning started almost as soon as the Civil War ended. Credit for the idea of Philadelphia hosting America's first world exposition generally goes to a college professor, John Campbell, who reportedly suggested it to the city's mayor, Morton McMichael, in 1866. The notion percolated for five years, but nothing was done. In 1871, a group of businessmen, led by department store owner John Wanamaker, teamed up with Republican Party officials and the Franklin Institute to petition Congress to authorize a centennial exposition and appoint a commission to get the project in motion. Congress agreed but only under the condition that all the money come from private sources and not the government.

For a time, it seemed as if the exposition would never come together. There were disagreements on where the fairgrounds should be, what should be the event's focus, and who should be in charge of seeing the project through to completion. When a panic hit the stock market in 1873, the economy crashed, and private money was nowhere to be found, the idea appeared to be dead. But the organizers were not going to be defeated that easily. For two years, they publicized the coming fair and went to everyone who might be able to contribute—church organizations, state governments, universities, major industries, and even foreign governments. Newspapers played up how important the centennial exposition was to national pride, and a women's committee sent members door-to-door and raised $100,000. The money from all these sources was enough to start construction but not finish it. In the end, the federal government was forced to make up the difference, although only on the condition that it was a loan, not an investment. That meant the government had to be paid back before any funds were returned to any actual investors. (It would take a Supreme Court ruling to enforce that agreement, and so most investors lost a good deal of money on the deal.)

Officially named the International Exhibition of Arts, Manufactures and Products of the Soil and Mine, the fair was colossal. The grounds covered 285 acres along the Schuylkill River, and contained more than 200 pavilions, with seven miles of avenues and walkways between them. On opening day, May 10, 1876, a troop of cavalry escorted President and Mrs. Grant to their places in the grandstand, along with Emperor Dom Pedro II and Empress Teresa of Brazil. An orchestra played the national anthems of a dozen foreign nations and ended with the "Centennial Inauguration March," written by the great German composer Richard Wagner. Almost 200,000 people witnessed the opening-day ceremonies, and more than ten million would visit before the fair closed in November. Most entered the grounds through the newly invented automatic turnstile after paying their fifty-cent admission fee.

Their money was not wasted. There were five main buildings. The Main Exhibition Building, made of wood, iron, and glass, was the largest in the world, almost five hundred feet wide and a third of a mile long. To cool the immense structure during the Philadelphia summer, a series of fountains had been placed inside. In Machinery Hall, only slightly smaller, the fifty-foot-tall Corliss steam engine, also the world's largest, was connected to more than two miles of pipe and five

View from a balloon of the Philadelphia Centennial fairgrounds.

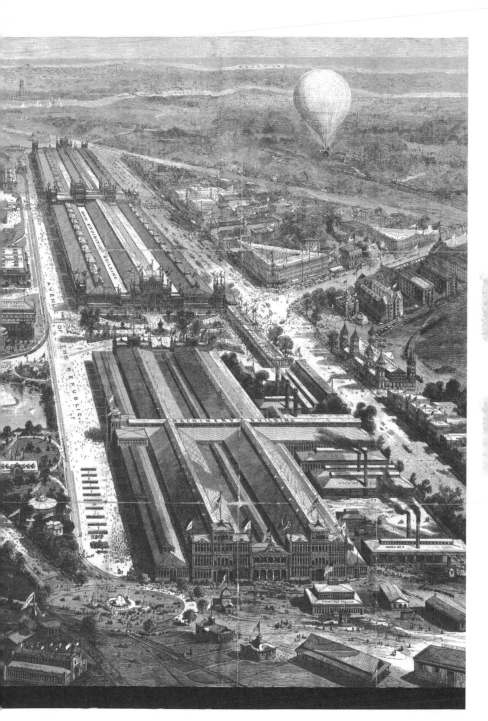

miles of overhead belts, which powered hundreds of other smaller machines on the exhibition floor. There was a Horticultural Hall, almost entirely glass-enclosed, devoted to plants, flowers, and garden design. Memorial Hall was filled with fine art, sculpture, and photography, and Agricultural Hall demonstrated modern farm equipment, while just outside was an immense exhibit dedicated to farming and livestock. A Women's Pavilion was also added when women protested that they had been ignored despite their enormous contribution to getting the fair off the ground.

Individual states, foreign nations, and businesses set up pavilions as well. Many Americans for the first time got to experience Heinz Ketchup, the Remington typewriter, the Singer sewing machine, and Hires Root Beer. Two other mechanical devices on display were to change the face of America and the world.

One was the bicycle. The model exhibited in Philadelphia was not the one we know today—the "safety bicycle," with both wheels of equal size—but rather the high-front-wheeled "ordinary" bicycle that most Americans now associate with circus performers. At the time, not only were there almost no bicycles in the United States, but also almost no roads on which to ride them. But one of the fair's visitors, Colonel Albert Augustus Pope, left Philadelphia with an idea. He not only redesigned the bicycle, making both wheels the same size, while changing the tires and the frame, but he also began a "Good Roads" movement to create places for people to ride.

President Grant and Emperor Dom Pedro starting the Corliss engine, which officially opened the fair.

It was a brilliant plan. During the next fifteen years, tens of millions of Pope's Columbia Chainless bicycles (and other brands) were sold in the United States. Bicycling not only became an appealing new way for gentlemen and ladies to spend time together, but women saw the freedom of cycling as a symbol of political freedom. By the mid-1880s, a woman on a bicycle became a badge of liberation. Famed suffragette Susan B. Anthony said, "The bicycle has done more for the emancipation of women than anything in the world."

The bicycle also inspired inventions of a more complex sort. Three of the men who used the device as a basis for other designs were Wilbur and Orville Wright, and Henry Ford. Almost every American inventor who was investigating the horseless carriage or controlled powered flight began on a bicycle.

The other device was called the Brayton Ready Motor. It featured a piston driven by a new fuel, kerosene, which was refined from petroleum. Soon, kerosene would give way to gasoline (at the time, used only as a stain remover), which became the source of power for both airplanes and automobiles. The Brayton motor was not used in either of these machines but became the basis decades later for jet engines.

During its six-month run, the Philadelphia Centennial Exposition showed the world that the United States, the land of democracy and freedom, had taken its place as a world power. The nation could justifiably brag of the great heights to which a free people could ascend.

Columbia Chainless.

In Louisiana, however, just as this great monument to American progress was being constructed on the banks of the Schuylkill, a different sort of America was taking shape.

When Joseph Bradley overturned the guilty verdicts of the three Colfax defendants, it did more than set three murderers free. It announced to white supremacists that they no longer need fear the federal court system, which meant they need not fear the courts at all.

Only weeks later, C. C. Nash, Johnnie Hadnot, and others from the Colfax raiding party joined together in a group they called the White Man's League. They celebrated its founding by murdering two local freedmen and trampling the crops of many others.

The idea spread quickly and soon the White League, as it was known, became a statewide organization. The two defense attorneys from the Colfax trial played major roles in ensuring this was no mere mob but rather a disciplined, military organization aimed at taking back state government by force.

Hugh J. Campbell, an ex-Union general from Iowa, explained the group's aims in an address to a Republican gathering in New Orleans in January 1875. "The Democratic and White League campaign of 1874 was a second edition of the White Camellia campaign of 1868. It opened by an organized, systematic plan, commenced simultaneously throughout the State, for ejecting by violence from their positions the lawfully appointed or elected parish officials, and substituting in their places the so-called McEnery officials. The opening act of this novel political campaign was the capture by a mob of six men, officials of Lincoln parish, two of whom held appointments under the United States, and their murder in cold blood. Not a solitary-conservative newspaper in this State has denounced this atrocity, while several of them have boldly and repeatedly applauded and endorsed it."

The White League launched a campaign of murder and intimidation across Louisiana. The only areas where African-Americans and white Republicans were safe were in those few places where the army maintained a serious presence. Even there, however, as support for the White League grew, it

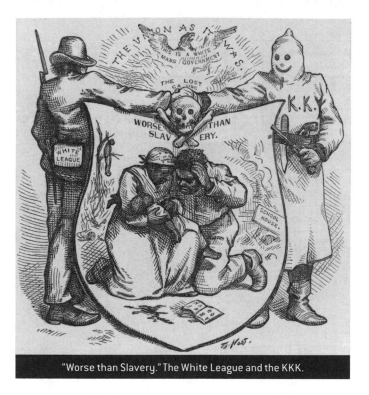

"Worse than Slavery." The White League and the KKK.

appeared that what had become an outnumbered force of federal troops would not be enough.

In September 1874, five thousand White League members descended on New Orleans to remove Governor Kellogg and install John McEnery as governor. In what became known as the Second Battle of Liberty Place, the White League succeeded in overwhelming a smaller force of police and militia, seizing the government, and ousting the governor. Dozens died. They held the city for three days until President Grant sent in troops to take the city back. An agreement was reached in which the White League retreated but none of the members would be prosecuted.

White Leaguers attacking the integrated police force during the Second Battle of Liberty Place.

The invaders were heroes to most of the population. In 1891, the city erected a monument honoring the sixteen White League members who were killed in the battle. In 1932, a plaque was added. It read, "McEnery and Penn having been elected governor and lieutenant-governor by the white people were duly installed by this overthrow of carpetbag government, ousting the usurpers, Governor Kellogg (white) and Lieutenant-Governor Antoine (colored). United States troops took over the state government and reinstated the usurpers but the national election of November 1876 recognized white supremacy in the South and gave us our state." The monument was removed from New Orleans in April 2017.

As late as 1966, New Orleans whites were celebrating the

battle as the "Overthrow of Carpet-Bag Rule in New Orleans." That year, a local man named Stuart Omer Landry produced a widely read pamphlet dedicated to "The Memory of the Heroes of the Fourteenth of September, whose Patriotism should be an Inspiration, not only to their Descendants, but to all Louisianans of Good Intent."

Although Supreme Court justices claim not to be influenced by public opinion or current events, the nine men on the Waite court were fully aware that Joseph Bradley's circuit court ruling had unleashed a wave of violence and murder in Louisiana that was, even as they prepared to hear *United States v. Cruikshank*, spreading like wildfire across the South.

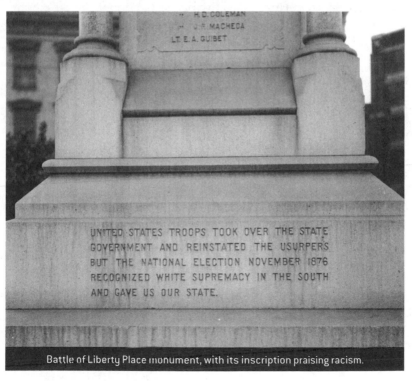

Battle of Liberty Place monument, with its inscription praising racism.

19

THE END OF THE LINE

A CASE BEFORE THE Supreme Court consists of two segments, argument and rebuttal. In the first, each side sets out why it thinks the verdict should be in its favor. The oral argument follows a brief, a written record of the argument that has been submitted to the justices in advance. In the next phase of the case, rebuttal, each side has the opportunity to state why the other side's argument was flawed, or why it did not correctly apply the law. Any justice can break in with questions at any point in the proceedings.

Appearing before the Supreme Court is as prestigious an activity as there is for a lawyer in the United States, so Attorney General George Williams decided to take over the case from J. R. Beckwith, his subordinate, and handle the rebuttal himself. That meant he would be questioned by eight men he had hoped he would be supervising, plus Morrison Waite, the man who had gotten the job instead. Williams faced an extremely difficult task. Not only had the government lost in circuit court, but it had lost to a man facing him on the bench. He would therefore either have to find a way to demonstrate to Justice Bradley that his opinion had been in error—and Bradley was not a man who admitted error readily—or persuade five of Bradley's colleagues of the same thing.

Williams employed an interesting and quite clever strategy. Although he discussed points of law and why he disagreed with Bradley's opinion, he spent a good deal of time reminding the justices that they were not simply deciding a legal debate, but ruling on a horrible, real-world crime—more than one hundred citizens of the United States had been murdered, shot down in cold blood, their bodies left to rot in the Louisiana sun. As it was, only three of more than one hundred fifty who participated in the slaughter had been brought to justice. If these three were freed, it would certainly—and had already—lead to more murders.

But there would be no quick decision in the case. After the arguments concluded, the Court adjourned to allow the justices to ride circuit, and that was followed by a summer recess. Even when the justices returned in October 1875, they did not issue an opinion.

At the same time they were deciding *Cruikshank*, the Court was also debating another case, *United States v. Reese*, in which an African-American man had been refused the right to vote because an official in Kentucky refused to accept his $1.50 poll tax. *Cruikshank* and *Reese* were to be Morrison Waite's first major cases on the Court, and he decided to write the opinions himself. It was not until March 27, 1876, five weeks before the centennial exposition would open in Philadelphia, that his decision was made public.

The Colfax defendants would go free.

To overturn the *Cruikshank* convictions, Waite, like Bradley, used technical flaws in Beckwith's indictment. But the larger issue was the Enforcement Acts themselves. Did the Fourteenth Amendment apply the Bill of Rights to the states as well as to the federal government? To the new chief justice, the answer was a firm no.

"The first amendment to the Constitution," Waite wrote, "prohibits Congress from abridging 'the right of the people to assemble and to petition the government for a redress of grievances.' This, like the other amendments proposed and adopted at the same time, *was not intended to limit the powers of the State governments in respect to their own citizens, but to operate upon the National Government alone.*"

Waite, also like Bradley, insisted that the federal government could only intervene if "new rights" had been created. Violations of "old rights" could not fall under federal law. Waite did agree that the Fifteenth Amendment created a "new right," the right not to be denied the vote "on account of race, color or previous condition of servitude." Congress, then, could indeed enforce the Fifteenth Amendment against the actions of private individuals, although only when *specifically* and *explicitly* stemming from racial discrimination. Having agreed to the same absurd test that Joseph Bradley had created, Waite then proceeded to agree with Bradley that, in *Cruikshank*, the test had not been passed. He ruled that although more than one hundred African-Americans had been hunted down and murdered by a mob of white men who had bragged about "killing niggers," the prosecution had failed to demonstrate that the attack was racially motivated. And so, after one of the most ghastly and barbaric incidents of mass murder in American history, not one single person was punished.

Waite came to a similar decision in *Reese*, and dismissed that suit as well.

Morrison Waite's Supreme Court had undone laws or amendments that Congress had passed, the president had signed, and the states had ratified. The justices, unelected and serving for life, had crafted a *new* law for the nation. As long as those who would deny the vote, employ terror, or even commit murder did not announce that their motives were racial, the federal government would be forced to sit by and watch it happen. The Fourteenth and Fifteenth Amendments were to be nothing but hollow shells.

That the Court had literally rewritten two constitutional amendments met with widespread public praise. Famed Supreme Court historian Charles Warren concluded that the *Cruikshank* and *Reese* decisions were "most fortunate," in that they "eliminated from politics the negro question which had so long embittered Congressional debates; they relegated the burden and duty of protecting the negro to the States, to whom they properly belonged." A newspaper claimed, "To assume State powers as the method of punishing and preventing wrongs in the State would be an experiment with our political system that had better be omitted. Southern questions, so far as they are State questions, must be left to the States themselves, and to those moral influences that finally shape the course of legislation. The General Government cannot authoritatively deal with them, without producing more evils than it will remedy."

Morrison Waite, the object of ridicule after his nomination, was now greatly admired for his courageous stand. The *New York Times* noted, "So far as the decisions can be regarded as reflecting on [Chief Justice Waite's] influence upon the court, they afford abundant evidence that his appointment was a judicious one, adding strength and dignity to the great tribunal over which he presides." Another editorial read, "Chief Justice Waite, in this decision and in the terms of its utterance has vindicated his disposition and his capacity to emulate the fame of Jay, Marshall, and Taney."

Once the Court had erected such impossible barriers to the protection of even the most fundamental constitutional rights of African-Americans, all that was left to prevent full restoration of white domination in the South was a fast-shrinking group of Radical Republicans in Congress and the army of occupation. Both would be gone within a year.

20

PRESIDENT BY ONE VOTE—
THE FIFTEENTH MAN

SEVEN MONTHS AFTER *Cruikshank* was decided, the nation went to the polls to elect a new president. The 1876 election between the Republican Rutherford B. Hayes and Democrat Samuel Tilden swung on two main issues: corruption in the Grant administration—Governor Tilden promoted his reputation as the man who had taken on New York's corrupt Tammany Hall and the notorious William Magear "Boss" Tweed—and whether the Reconstruction state governments in the old Confederacy would continue or fall to white rule.

Hayes, trying to win as a Republican in a nation shifting to Democrats, ran as a friend to black Americans, pledging to maintain the social advances of Reconstruction against Redeemer movements. But he also courted white votes in the North—and the South—by painting the Democrats as the party that had wished to destroy the nation. Former Chief Justice William Rehnquist observed that Hayes's tactic was "to impress on the electorate that while every Democrat had not been a rebel, every rebel had been a Democrat." Tilden, on the other hand, "appealed to those throughout the country who were fed up with the corrupt mess in Washington, and to white Southerners who sought to recapture the control of their state governments from Republican carpetbaggers and from newly free African Americans."

Neither side addressed the need to stem the increasing violence in the Southern states. Even with the constant protection of the army, the possibility that a Reconstruction state government might be overthrown by armed rebellion had become a real possibility. The only choices to avoid that seemed to be toughening the military presence and making the army a true occupying force, or pulling the troops out, leaving the South to Redeemers, and blacks and their supporters to their fates.

When the ballots were counted, Tilden had easily won the popular vote and could solidly claim 184 electoral votes, one less than the number needed for election. Hayes could claim only 165 electoral votes. Twenty electoral votes were in dispute, 19 of which were in the three Reconstruction states still officially under Republican control: Florida, Louisiana, and South Carolina. The other vote was from Oregon, which Hayes seemed to have won. In each of the three Southern states, Tilden appeared to have won the popular vote, but reports of voter intimidation and fraud were widespread. If even one of these disputed electoral votes went to Tilden—and he certainly seemed entitled to some of them—he would win the presidency.

Rutherford B. Hayes.

Almost every newspaper in America reported Tilden as the winner. But not the *New York Times*. On November 6, the day before the election, the newspaper had proclaimed, "Republican Success Certain." The *Times*'s managing editor, John C. Reid, had been held as a prisoner of war at the infamous Andersonville prison during the Civil War, and he loathed Democrats. Reid spent election night convincing New York Republican leaders not to give up, that Tilden might not have won the election after all. When he was done, the New Yorkers telegraphed Republicans in the disputed states and told them to hold out, to challenge the results.

The *Times* did its bit by announcing, "Result Still Uncertain," on November 8. On November 9, two days after Election Day, the paper ran a page-one headline: "The Battle Won. Governor Hayes Elected—The Republicans Carry Twenty-one States, Casting 185 Electoral Votes." To get to 185, the *Times* had awarded the Louisiana, Florida, and South Carolina electors to

"Tilden or Blood." Political cartoon about the disputed election of 1876.

Hayes. The article claimed to have based its statement on canvasses—checks of the results—although the *Times* was vague on just who had done the canvassing.

Canvassing boards were indeed appointed in each state by the sitting Republican governments, although not until after the *Times* ran its piece. Not surprisingly, the canvassing board in each state, ignoring the reported vote totals, confirmed what the *Times* had said and declared Hayes the winner. While fraud and dirty tricks were rampant on both sides, "Tilden was almost certainly the rightful winner in Louisiana, probably the victor in Florida . . . and perhaps the winner in South Carolina, too." Of course, in each of those states, the

Republican vote was kept down because many black men feared to try to go to the polls.

Democrats howled fraud. Threats of armed revolt spread throughout Washington. Calls for secession were heard for the first time since the war. A shot was fired at Hayes's home in Ohio while the candidate was having dinner inside.

The Constitution did not provide for this sort of situation, but *some* solution had to be devised. The two parties agreed to appoint a fifteen-man Electoral Commission: five senators, five representatives, and five Supreme Court justices. Seven would be Democrats, seven Republicans, and the fifteenth nonpartisan—a man who each side agreed would vote only on merit and not by party. It was easy to see that the fifteenth man would in effect choose the president by himself. In a country so divided, after an election so bitter, finding that one fair and honest man might have seemed impossible.

But incredibly, such a man seemed both to exist and to be available. Associate Justice of the Supreme Court David Davis, a Lincoln appointee, was acceptable to both sides. So trusted as an independent was the justice that it was said, "No one, perhaps not even Davis himself, knew which presidential candidate he preferred."

But before the commission could meet, the Democratic-controlled state legislature in Illinois appointed Davis to a vacant seat in the United States Senate. Republican newspapers denounced the gesture as an obvious attempt at flattery.

Both sides assumed Davis would decline the seat and remain on the Court, but Republicans feared the honor of being named by Democrats might tip his vote toward Tilden. Davis took care of that by immediately resigning from the bench to accept the appointment. He never stated his reasons for leaving both the Court and the commission, but perhaps the huge responsibility of choosing a president was more than he could handle.

With Davis, perhaps the only acceptable independent in the entire nation, now ineligible, one of the remaining four justices would be forced to sit in his place. Each was associated with one of the political parties. Eventually, also for reasons never made public, recently appointed Associate Justice Joseph Bradley was chosen to take Davis's place. Democrats called the choice a fix, but after trying to bribe Davis, they had lost the ability to mount a serious challenge. Bradley accepted the appointment and became the only man in American history empowered to choose a president essentially on his own.

Ever meticulous, Bradley composed a detailed written opinion, what lawyers call a "brief," for each man, trying to prove why he was the real winner. Associates insisted that he went only on the facts, judging each party's claim fairly and with care.

Then, to no one's surprise, Joseph Bradley accepted every argument made by Republicans and chose Hayes. Democrats were furious and some threatened rebellion. Rumors circulated that an army of 100,000 men was prepared to march on the

A Democratic poster denouncing the Compromise of 1877. The illustration is titled: "The Ten White Men and Two Negroes Who Defrauded the American People out of their Choice for President in 1876."

capital to prevent "Rutherfraud" or "His Fraudulency" from being sworn in. In the House of Representatives, Democrats began a filibuster to prevent Hayes's inauguration.

What happened next has been a subject of debate among historians ever since. The simplest explanation is the most widely accepted. "Reasonable men in both parties struck a bargain at Wormley's Hotel. There, in the traditional smoke-filled room, emissaries of Hayes agreed to abandon the Republican state governments in Louisiana and South Carolina while southern Democrats agreed to abandon the filibuster and thus trade off the presidency in exchange for the end of Reconstruction." The Compromise of 1877, as it came to be known, made Rutherford B. Hayes the nineteenth president of the United States. As one of his first orders of business, this supposed defender of African-American rights ordered federal troops withdrawn from the South. When the soldiers marched out, they took Reconstruction with them.

EPILOGUE

UNPUNISHED MURDER

THE SUPREME COURT'S DECISION in *United States v. Cruikshank* did not doom the struggle for equal rights by itself. But it did start America on the path to what would become known as Jim Crow, a society in which black Americans, full citizens of this nation, were condemned to a system that was slavery in all but name. And once on that disgraceful path, the Supreme Court would rule again and again, under a legal philosophy called "strict construction"—choosing language over justice— that the right of African-American citizens to vote, to be treated as equals under the law, or even to remain free, could be trampled on by any state government that so chose.

Those involved in the Colfax Massacre and the trials that came afterward had widely different fates. J. R. Beckwith, who had tried with such passion and commitment to gain justice for the victims, was forced from his job by Rutherford B. Hayes, the man who had proclaimed himself a defender of equal rights. Beckwith remained in New Orleans and practiced law until his death in 1912.

William Woods, the judge who had been frustrated when Joseph Bradley took over his trial and freed the defendants, became Bradley's colleague when he was appointed to the Supreme Court by the same Rutherford B. Hayes in 1881. But Woods was no longer the same man he had been during the Colfax trials. Once on the court, he would author another of the Court's shameful civil rights opinions, this one overturning the conviction of twenty Klan members who had murdered a black man. It was unconstitutional, he wrote, for the federal government to prosecute "ordinary" crimes, such as murder—only local governments could do that. Woods defended his decision using the same strict-construction reasoning that Joseph Bradley had used to void the convictions in the Colfax cases.

Joseph Bradley remained on the Court until 1892, his racist views becoming more and more obvious while at the same time his reputation as a brilliant legal mind increased. In 1883, he would write the opinion in the *Civil Rights Cases*, which declared the Civil Rights Act of 1875 unconstitutional. He was praised in both the North and the South for upholding individual liberty.

Morrison Waite would serve as chief justice until his death in 1888, presiding over a court that had steadily destroyed the hopes and dreams of black Americans in the South. In 1886, he would declare that corporations were legally "people," and had therefore earned the very Fourteenth Amendment protections he had denied freedmen.

The invaders in the Colfax Massacre went on to live prosperous lives, none more so than C. C. Nash. Nash married well, bought land, and became a wealthy man. He and the other participants went on to be celebrated as heroes in Jim Crow Louisiana. After Nash died in his bed at age eighty-six on June 29, 1922, his obituary in a Louisiana newspaper read, "With the sounding of Taps, the last solemn requiem, all that was mortal of Captain C. C. Nash was laid away, with military honors Friday morning, Company C., as guard of honor, escorting the remains of the old Confederate soldier to the grave, firing the last salute. Capt. Nash, who was in his 86th year, not only took a prominent part in the affairs of his nation during the Civil War, when he won honors and distinction for bravery, but was a conspicuous figure during the Reconstruction period, being one of the few remaining heroes of the historical Colfax riot episode."

In 1921, to commemorate the incident at Colfax, citizens and the government of Grant Parish donated money to erect a twelve-foot obelisk in a local cemetery, inscribed "In loving remembrance" to the three "heroes" who had fallen in the "Colfax riot, fighting for white supremacy." In 1950, the state of Louisiana erected a plaque memorializing the spot that "marked the end of carpetbag misrule in the South."

The victims, however, received quite different treatment. The bodies of at least two dozen of the murdered men had not been buried until the troops arrived days after the killing. The soldiers were forced to bury the rotting corpses in a common grave. Almost a century later, black construction workers excavating near the site discovered human bones in the earth they had cleared away. None of the remains could be identified.

Colfax plaque.

GLOSSARY

Amendment: An addition to the Constitution that either clarified a passage that had not been precise, changed the powers of the federal government—usually by expanding them—or limited the power of the states to enact certain types of laws.

Anti-Federalist: Someone who opposed the Constitution, usually because it gave too much power to the new national (federal) government. Anti-Federalists failed to prevent ratification of the Constitution, but many later became supporters of Thomas Jefferson, who favored the states retaining more power. People with this point of view later evolved into states' rights supporters, many of whom also either supported or accepted slavery.

Appeal: An attempt to retry a case in a higher court after an unfavorable verdict.

Appellate jurisdiction: A court that has the power to hear appeals of a verdict given in a different court.

Articles of Confederation: The governing document of the United States before ratification of the Constitution. The states had much more power under the Articles, so much so that the United States often functioned more like thirteen separate nations than one.

Bill of Rights: The first ten amendments to the Constitution, adopted by the 1st Congress. Most amendments laid out rights of individuals or how the federal government could or could not limit those rights. The Tenth Amendment limited the powers of the federal government with respect to state governments.

Black Codes: Laws passed after the Civil War by white-dominated governments of former Confederate states that denied African-Americans basic rights of citizenship.

Carpetbagger: A Northerner who came south after the Civil War. Many Southerners accused these people of trying only to make money or gain power in the defeated Confederacy, while others believed most came to help integrate the freed slaves into mainstream society.

Circuit court: The middle layer of the federal judiciary. Circuit courts are mostly appellate, ruling on cases in which the loser in district court seeks a different ruling.

Defendant: Someone accused of a crime or misdeed.

Democratic Party: A states' rights political party begun by Andrew Jackson after his loss in the presidential election of 1824, in which he got more popular and electoral votes than either of his opponents.

District court: The lowest layer of the federal court system. District courts take any case in which a plaintiff can demonstrate that the action comes under federal law.

Electoral College: The body that actually chooses the president of the United States. Electors are chosen by states, each state having electors equal to the total number of its representatives and senators.

Enforcement Acts: Laws passed by Congress during Reconstruction to ensure that the provisions of the Fourteenth and Fifteenth Amendments were adhered to in the conquered South.

Federalist: Someone who favored ratifying the Constitution, and later a member of the political party of the first two presidents, George Washington and John Adams, as well as Chief Justice John Marshall. Federalists generally favored a stronger national (federal) government with less power reserved for state governments.

Freedmen: Freed slaves.

Freedmen's Bureau: An organization created by Congress to help freedmen join mainstream society. It provided food, clothing, medical services, education, and other essentials.

Fusionists: A political party or movement that is a blend of other parties that had previously been adversaries.

Grand jury: A panel of citizens whose role is to decide if there is enough evidence to indict (bring to trial) someone accused of a crime.

Indictment: An official accusation issued by a grand jury or a judge to bring to trial a person or persons said to have committed a crime.

Judicial review: The power of a federal court to declare a law unconstitutional. The final decision on constitutionality will almost always be made by the Supreme Court.

Judiciary: A system of courts.

Missouri Compromise: An 1820 agreement in Congress that attempted to balance admission of new slave and free states, and to set the boundary of where slavery would be permitted in the United States.

Parish: What a county is called in Louisiana.

Petit jury (or simply "jury"): A panel that decides whether the plaintiff or defendant wins, often the guilt or innocence of the defendant.

Plaintiff: The party bringing a lawsuit or making an accusation.

Quorum: The minimum number of legislators required to be present in order to vote on a measure.

Radical Republicans: Congressmen after the Civil War who insisted that the United States accept freed slaves fully and completely as citizens and punish anyone in the former Confederacy who opposed that aim.

Ratification: Agreement to adopt a document or plan, usually by vote.

Reconstruction: A program to integrate freed slaves into ordinary society and to protect their rights as citizens. An important part of Reconstruction was to specify the conditions under which Confederate states could rejoin the Union.

Reconstruction Acts: Laws passed by Congress to set the conditions under which former Confederate states could rejoin the Union and also to ensure that states in the old Confederacy did not abuse the rights of their new black citizens. One of the acts divided the Confederacy into five military districts, each under the command of an army general.

Redeemer: Someone who, after the Civil War, wanted to return the South to the same social structure as before the war. If African-Americans could no longer be slaves, they would be treated in the "Redeemed" South as slaves in everything but name. Some Redeemer groups turned to violence, such as the Kuklux, later called the Ku Klux Klan, and the Knights of the White Camellia.

Republican Party: A political party formed in the 1850s to oppose the expansion of slavery. Their first candidate for president was Abraham Lincoln in 1860.

Scalawag: A Southerner during Reconstruction who seemed sympathetic to Northern views and sought to destroy traditional Southern society, based in white supremacy.

Supreme Court: The highest court in the United States, the top layer of the federal judiciary. The Supreme Court consists of a chief justice and, since 1869, a fixed number of eight associate justices. The Supreme Court's jurisdiction is almost exclusively appellate, although there are some rare instances when cases will begin there, called original jurisdiction.

Trial: A court proceeding in which a decision is reached that favors either the plaintiff or the defendant. In some cases, in a "mistrial" or a "hung jury," no decision is reached and the trial must be conducted again.

Underground Railroad: A network of abolitionists who would either smuggle slaves out of the South or protect runaways who had made their way to the North. The "railroad" consisted of a series of "stations" (safe houses) where slaves were hidden until they could safely leave for a part of America where slave catchers could not function, or sometimes for Canada.

Verdict: A decision in a court case. A verdict can be rendered, or announced, by a jury, a judge, or sometimes a panel of judges.

White League: A military white supremacist organization, formed in Colfax after the *Cruikshank* decision, whose stated purpose was to reinstitute white rule in Louisiana by force.

BIBLIOGRAPHY

ONLINE RESOURCES

"Appletons' Annual Cyclopaedia and Register of Important Events of the Year 1865: Embracing Political, Military, and Ecclesiastical Affairs; Public Documents; Biography, Statistics, Commerce, Finance, Literature, Science, Agriculture, and Mechanical Industry." Vol. 5. New York: D. Appleton, 1870. https://catalog .hathitrust.org/Record/010032198

"Circuit Court of the United States. District of Louisiana. The *United States v. Cruikshank* et al." *The American Law Register* (1852–1891), Vol. 22, No. 10, New Series Volume 13 (Oct., 1874). https://www.jstor.org/stable/3303600?seq=1#page _scan_tab_contents

"The Strange Career of 'State Action' under the Fifteenth Amendment." *Yale Law Journal*, Vol. 74, No. 8 (Jul., 1965). https://www.jstor.org/stable/794732?scq=1#page _scan_tab_contents

"The White League Conspiracy against Free Government." Speech delivered by Hugh J. Campbell, 1875. Privately printed pamphlet. https://archive.org/details /whiteleagueconsp00camp

Brooklyn Daily Eagle. Brooklyn Newstand, a website of Brooklyn Public Library. https://bklyn.newspapers.com

Chronicling America: Historic American Newspapers. http://chroniclingamerica .loc.gov

Congressional Globe. https://memory.loc.gov/ammem/amlaw/lwcg.html

Congressional Record. https://memory.loc.gov/ammem/amlaw/lwcr.html

New York Times. https://www.nytimes.com/

Statutes at Large. https://memory.loc.gov/ammem/amlaw/lwsl.html

United States Reports. http://loc.heinonline.org/loc/LOC?index=usreportsloc

BOOKS AND ARTICLES

Abraham, Harry J. "John Marshall Harlan: A Justice Neglected." *Virginia Law Review*, Vol. 41, No. 7 (Nov., 1955).

Benedict, Michael Les. "Preserving Federalism: Reconstruction and the Waite Court." *Supreme Court Review*, Vol. 1978 (1978).

Borchard, Edwin. "The Supreme Court and Private Rights." *Yale Law Journal*, Vol. 47, No. 7 (May, 1938).

Branch, Mary Polk. *Memoirs of a Southern Woman*. Chicago: Joseph E. Branch Publishing Company, 1912.

"Brutus." "To the people of New York." *New York Journal*, March 20, 1788. http://teachingamericanhistory.org/library/document/brutus-xv/

Bryant-Jones, Mildred. "The Political Program of Thaddeus Stevens, 1865." *Phylon*, Vol. 2, No. 2 (2nd Qtr., 1941).

Burton, Thomas W. *What Experience Has Taught Me: An Autobiography of Thomas William Burton*. Cincinnati: Press of Jennings and Graham, 1910.

Champagne, Anthony, and Dennis Pope. "Joseph P. Bradley: An Aspect of a Judicial Personality." *Political Psychology*, Vol. 6, No. 3 (Sep., 1985).

Corwin, Edward S. "The Supreme Court and the Fourteenth Amendment." *Michigan Law Review*, Vol. 7, No. 8 (Jun., 1909).

Currie, David P. "The Constitution in the Supreme Court: Civil War and Reconstruction, 1865–1873." *University of Chicago Law Review*, Vol. 51, No. 1 (Winter, 1984).

Dethloff, Henry C., and Robert R. Jones. "Race Relations in Louisiana, 1877–98." *Louisiana History: Journal of the Louisiana Historical Association*, Vol. 9, No. 4 (Autumn, 1968).

Douglass, Frederick. *Frederick Douglass: Selected Speeches and Writings*, edited by Philip S. Foner and Yuval Taylor. Chicago: Chicago Review Press, 2000.

Du Bois, W. E. B. "Reconstruction and Its Benefits." *American Historical Review*, Vol. 15, No. 4 (Jul., 1910).

———. "Reconstruction, Seventy-Five Years After." *Phylon*, Vol. 4, No. 3 (3rd Qtr., 1943).

Epps, Garrett. *Democracy Reborn: The Fourteenth Amendment and the Fight for Equal Rights in Post-Civil War America*. New York: Henry Holt, 2006.

Fairman, Charles. "Mr. Justice Bradley's Appointment to the Supreme Court and the Legal Tender Cases." *Harvard Law Review*, Vol. 54, No. 6 (Apr., 1941), and Vol. 54, No. 7 (May, 1941).

Farrand, Max. *Records of the Federal Convention*. New Haven: Yale University Press, 1937.

Field, Henry M. *Blood Is Thicker than Water: A Few Days among Our Southern Brethren*. New York: George Munro, 1886.

Foner, Eric. *Reconstruction: America's Unfinished Revolution, 1863-1877*. New York: Harper and Row, 1988.

———. "Reconstruction Revisited." *Reviews in American History*, Vol. 10, No. 4, The Promise of American History: Progress and Prospects (Dec., 1982).

Franklin, John Hope. *Race and History: Selected Essays 1938-1988*. Baton Rouge, LA: Louisiana State University Press, 1989.

———. "'Legal' Disfranchisement of the Negro." *Journal of Negro Education*, Vol. 26, No. 3, The Negro Voter in the South (Summer, 1957).

Goff, John S. "The Rejection of United States Supreme Court Appointments." *American Journal of Legal History*, Vol. 5, No. 4 (Oct., 1961).

Hamilton, Alexander, James Madison, and John Jay. *The Federalist.* http://avalon .law.yale.edu/subject_menus/fed.asp

H. M. J. "Federal Jurisdiction: The Civil Rights Removal Statute Revisited." *Duke Law Journal*, Vol. 16, No. 1 (Feb., 1967).

Horan, Michael J. "Political Economy and Sociological Theory as Influences upon Judicial Policy-Making: The Civil Rights Cases of 1883." *American Journal of Legal History*, Vol. 16, No. 1 (Jan., 1972).

Kaminski, John P., Gaspare J. Saladino, et al., eds. *The Documentary History of the Ratification of the Constitution.* Vol.X. Madison: Wisconsin Historical Society, 1990, 1993.

Keith, LeeAnna. *The Colfax Massacre: The Untold Story of Black Power, White Terror, and the Death of Reconstruction.* New York: Oxford University Press, 2008.

Klarman, Michael J. *From Jim Crow to Civil Rights: The Supreme Court and the Struggle for Racial Equality.* New York: Oxford University Press, 2004.

Kutler, Stanley I. "Reconstruction and the Supreme Court: The Numbers Game Reconsidered." *Journal of Southern History*, Vol. 32, No. 1 (Feb., 1966).

———. *Judicial Power and Reconstruction Politics.* Chicago: University of Chicago Press, 1968.

Lackner, Joseph H. "The Foundation of St. Ann's Parish, 1866–1870: The African-American Experience in Cincinnati." *U.S. Catholic Historian*, Vol. 14, No. 2, Parishes and Peoples: Religious and Social Meanings, Part One (Spring, 1996).

Lane, Charles. *The Day Freedom Died: The Colfax Massacre, the Supreme Court, and the Betrayal of Reconstruction.* New York: Henry Holt and Company, 2008.

Levy, Leonard W. *Original Intent and the Framers' Constitution.* New York: Macmillan, 1988.

Litwack, Leon F. *Trouble in Mind: Black Southerners in the Age of Jim Crow.* New York: Alfred A. Knopf, 1998.

Lynd, Staughton. "Rethinking Slavery and Reconstruction." *Journal of Negro History*, Vol. 50, No. 3 (Jul., 1965).

Magliocca, Gerard N. *American Founding Son: John Bingham and the Invention of the Fourteenth Amendment.* New York: NYU Press, 2016.

McPherson, James M. "Abolitionists and the Civil Rights Act of 1875." *Journal of American History*, Vol. 52, No. 3 (Dec., 1965).

Montgomery, Frank Alexander. *Reminiscences of a Mississippian in Peace and War.* Cincinnati: Robert Clarke Company, 1901.

Morris, Roy, Jr., *Fraud of the Century. Rutherford B. Hayes, Samuel Tilden, and the Stolen Election of 1876.* New York: Simon and Schuster, 2003.

Nagle, John C. "How Not to Count Votes." *Columbia Law Review*, Vol. 104, No. 6 (Oct., 2004).

Nardini, Louis R., Sr. "A Grant Parish History." *Colfax Chronicle*, August 24, 1962.

Nimmer, Melville B. "A Proposal for Judicial Validation of a Previously Unconstitutional Law: The Civil Rights Act of 1875." *Columbia Law Review*, Vol. 65, No. 8 (Dec., 1965).

Packard, Jerrold M. *American Nightmare: The History of Jim Crow*. New York: St. Martin's Press, 2002.

Peskin, Allan. "Was There a Compromise of 1877?" *Journal of American History*, Vol. 60, No. 1 (Jun., 1973).

Ratner, Sidney. "Was the Supreme Court Packed by President Grant?" *Political Science Quarterly*, Vol. 50, No. 3 (Sep., 1935).

Rehnquist, William H. *Centennial Crisis: The Disputed Election of 1876*. New York: Alfred A. Knopf, 2004.

Rosen, Jeffrey. *The Supreme Court: The Personalities and Rivalries That Defined America*. New York: Henry Holt, 2006.

Scovel, James M. "Thaddeus Stevens." *Lippincott's Monthly Magazine*, April 1898.

Shapiro, Samuel. "A Black Senator from Mississippi: Blanche K. Bruce." *Review of Politics*, Vol. 44, No. 1 (Jan., 1982).

Smith, George P. "Republican Reconstruction and Section Two of the Fourteenth Amendment." *Western Political Quarterly*, Vol. 23, No. 4 (Dec., 1970).

Smith, Walter George. "Roger Brooke Taney." *American Law Register*, Vol. 47, No. 4 (Apr., 1899).

Spackman, S. G. F. "American Federalism and the Civil Rights Act of 1875." *Journal of American Studies*, Vol. 10, No. 3 (Dec., 1976).

Stampp, Kenneth M. *The Era of Reconstruction 1865–1877*. New York: Alfred A. Knopf, 1965.

Tap, Bruce. *The Fort Pillow Massacre: North, South, and the Status of African-Americans in the Civil War Era*. New York: Routledge USA, 2013.

Trefousse, Hans L. *Andrew Johnson: A Biography*. New York: W. W. Norton, 1997.

Van Alstyne, William W. "The Fourteenth Amendment, the 'Right' to Vote, and the Understanding of the Thirty-Ninth Congress." *Supreme Court Review*, Vol. 1965 (1965).

Warren, Charles. *The Supreme Court in United States History, Volume 3*. Boston: Little, Brown and Company, 1922.

Weaver, Valeria W. "The Failure of Civil Rights 1875–1883 and Its Repercussions." *Journal of Negro History*, Vol. 54, No. 4 (Oct., 1969).

Westin, Alan F. "John Marshall Harlan and the Constitutional Rights of Negroes: The Transformation of a Southerner." *Yale Law Journal*, Vol. 66, No. 5 (Apr., 1957).

Wiecek, William M. "Emergence of Equality as a Constitutional Value: The First Century." *Chicago-Kent Law Review*, Vol. 82, No. 1 (2007).

Williams, George H. "Reminiscences of the United States Supreme Court." *Yale Law Journal*, Vol. 8, No. 7 (Apr., 1899).

Wilson, Woodrow. "The Reconstruction of the Southern States." *Atlantic Monthly*, Vol. 87 (Jan., 1901).

Woodburn, James Albert. *The Life of Thaddeus Stevens: A Study in American Political History, Especially in the Period of the Civil War and Reconstruction*. New York: Bobbs, Merrill, 1913.

Woodward, C. Vann. *The Burden of Southern History*. Baton Rouge, LA: Louisiana State University Press, 1968.

———. *The Strange Career of Jim Crow*. 2nd ed. New York: Oxford University Press, 1966.

———. *Origins of the New South, 1877–1913*. Baton Rouge, LA: Louisiana State University Press, 1951.

Wyatt-Brown, Bertram. "The Civil Rights Act of 1875." *The Western Political Quarterly*, Vol. 18, No. 4 (Dec., 1965).

SOURCE NOTES

Prologue

"It now appears . . ." *New York Times,* April 17, 1873, p. 1.

"The details of the massacre . . ." *NYT,* April 18, 1873, p. 4. (hereafter *NYT*)

"the largest circulation . . ." *Brooklyn Daily Eagle,* April 16, 1873, p. 2. (hereafter *BDE*)

Chapter 1

"The real difference . . ." Madison to the Federal Convention, July 14, 1787.

"They'll take your niggers . . ." John P. Kaminski and Gaspare J. Saladino, eds., *The Documentary History of the Ratification of the Constitution,* vol.X (Madison: Wisconsin Historical Society, 1990, 1993). Henry's pronouncement was reportedly met with laughter.

"I question whether . . ." "Brutus," "To the people of New York" (Anti-federalist XV), *New York Journal,* March 20, 1788.

"the weakest of the three." Alexander Hamilton, James Madison, and John Jay, *The Federalist.*

Chapter 2

"Judiciary Act of 1789 . . ." An Act to establish the Judicial Courts of the United States, Statutes at Large, 1 Stat. 73.

"say what the law is . . ." *Marbury v. Madison,* 5 U. S. 137 (1 Cranch 137).

Chapter 3

"John Marshall has made . . ." Most historians now think the quote was made up. But it certainly represented Jackson's view.

"My system was put . . ." Walter George Smith, "Roger Brooke Taney," *American Law Register,* Vol. 47, No. 4, Volume 38, p. 209.

"A hard necessity . . ." ibid, p. 211.

"had for more than a century . . ." *Dred Scott v. Sandford,* 60 U.S. 393 (1856).

"regarded, throughout the Free States . . ." *Chicago Daily Tribune,* March 13, 1857.

"the sanction of the . . ." *Mercury,* April 2, 1857.

"It is clearly not . . ." Frederick Douglass, *Frederick Douglass: Selected Speeches and Writings,* ed. Philip S. Foner and Yuval Taylor (Chicago: Chicago Review Press, 2000), p. 351.

"History will expose . . ." Philadelphia *North American,* October 14, 1864.

"a man of pure . . ." *NYT,* October 14, 1864, p. 4.

Chapter 4

"The lands in the hands . . ." *NYT,* December 6, 1865, p. 4.

"We hold this to be . . ." "Appletons' Annual Cyclopaedia and Register of Important Events of the Year 1865: Embracing Political, Military, and Ecclesiastical Affairs;

Public Documents; Biography, Statistics, Commerce, Finance, Literature, Science, Agriculture, and Mechanical Industry," Vol. 5 (New York: D. Appleton, 1870), p. 512.

"If anything can be proved . . ." Andrew Johnson, "Third Annual Message," December 3, 1867. Online by Gerhard Peters and John T. Woolley, The American Presidency Project, http://www.presidency.ucsb.edu/ws/?pid=29508.

"Strip a proud nobility . . ." James Albert Woodburn, *The Life of Thaddeus Stevens: A Study in American Political History, Especially in the Period of the Civil War and Reconstruction* (New York: Bobbs, Merrill, 1913), p. 362.

"Before I would see . . ." Hans L. Trefousse, *Andrew Johnson: A Biography* (New York: W. W. Norton, 1997), p. 166.

"No government can be free . . ." Stevens in a speech to the House of Representatives, January 3, 1867, http://www.bartleby.com/400/prose/906.html.

"The greatest measure . . ." "Thaddeus Stevens," *Lippincott's Monthly Magazine,* January 1898, p. 550.

"We have turned . . ." *Congressional Globe,* December 18, 1865.

"It is intended . . ." C. Vann Woodward, *The Burden of Southern History* (Baton Rouge, LA: Louisiana State University Press, 1968), p. 92.

"Slavery is dead . . ." Joseph H. Lackner, "The Foundation of St. Ann's Parish, 1866–1870: The African-American Experience in Cincinnati," *U.S. Catholic Historian,* Vol. 14, No. 2, Parishes and Peoples: Religious and Social Meanings, Part One (Spring, 1996), p. 14.

Chapter 5

"A Bill to Protect . . ." Civil Rights Act of 1866, Statutes at Large, 14 Stat. 27–30.

Chapter 6

"based upon the equality . . ." Gerard N. Magliocca, *American Founding Son: John Bingham and the Invention of the Fourteenth Amendment* (New York: NYU Press, 2016), p. 56.

"He was the saddest man . . ." ibid., p. 81.

"a simple, strong, plain declaration . . ." ibid., p. 125.

"protect all persons . . ." Statutes at Large, 39th Congress, 2nd Session, p. 428.

"were being trodden . . ." Johnson said those words to *New York Evening Post* editor Charles Nordhoff, who related them in a letter to William Cullen Bryant. Trefousse, p. 279.

Chapter 7

"The slaughter was awful . . ." Letter from Achilles Clark to his sister, April 14, 1864, quoted in Bruce Tap, *The Fort Pillow Massacre: North, South, and the Status of African-Americans in the Civil War Era* (New York: Routledge USA, 2013), p. 201.

"Then came Reconstruction days . . ." Mary Polk Branch, *Memoirs of a Southern Woman* (Chicago: Joseph E. Branch Publishing Company, 1912), p. 49.

"The sermon had commenced . . ." Thomas W. Burton, *What Experience Has Taught Me: An Autobiography of Thomas William Burton* (Cincinnati: Press of Jennings and Graham, 1910) pp. 27–28.

Chapter 8

"Mrs. Harriet Jacobs was sent . . ." *The Freedmen's Record* (Boston: New England Freedmen's Aid Society, February 1865), p. 19.

"The negroes stood . . ." Frank Alexander Montgomery. *Reminiscences of a Mississippian in Peace and War* (Cincinnati: Robert Clarke Company, 1901), pp. 268–270.

"He lived and breathed . . ." Philadelphia *Evening Telegraph*, August 12, 1868, p. 1.

"Evil Genius . . ." *NYT*, August 12, 1868, p. 4.

"intolerance of opposition . . ." *BDE*, August 13, 1868, p. 2.

"I have achieved nothing . . ." *Hartford Courant*, August 15, 1868, p. 1.

Chapter 10

"Thus Grant too . . ." Louis R. Nardini, Sr., "A Grant Parish History," *Colfax Chronicle*, August 24, 1962.

"The negroes of Colfax . . ." *Louisiana Democrat*, April 9, 1873, p. 2.

"At all events . . ." *New Orleans Republican*, April 8, 1873, p. 4. (hereafter *NOR*)

Chapter 11

"An extraordinary and very perilous state . . ." Woodrow Wilson, "The Reconstruction of the Southern States," *Atlantic Monthly*, Vol. 87 (Jan., 1901), pp. 6–7.

"kind and considerate man . . ." Samuel Shapiro. "A Black Senator from Mississippi: Blanche K. Bruce," *Review of Politics*, Vol. 44, No. 1 (Jan., 1982), p. 83.

"After the firing . . ." ibid., pp. 84–85.

"It will not accord . . ." *Congressional Record*, Vol. 1, part 1, 44th Congress, 1st Session (Washington, DC: Government Printing Office, 1876).

Chapter 12

"We want that courthouse . . ." Interview of C. C. Nash by T. W. DeKlyne, *Horrible Massacre in Grant Parish: Details of the Occurrence*, privately printed pamphlet (New Orleans, 1873), p. 26.

"A colored man . . ." ibid., p. 24.

"When forced by the fire . . ." ibid.

"Mr. Nash stated . . ." ibid, p. 26.

"It is asserted . . ." ibid., pp. 24–25.

"I didn't come four hundred miles . . ." *NOR*, February 28, 1874, p. 5.

"Mr. R. G. Hill . . ." *NOR*, April 16, 1873, p. 1.

Chapter 13

"Several times, after their evening drill . . ." *Louisiana Democrat*, April 23, 1873, p. 1.

"If two or more persons . . ." Statutes at Large, 16 Stat. 140–146 (1870).

"spare no pains or expense . . ." Quoted in Charles Lane, *The Day Freedom Died: The Colfax Massacre, the Supreme Court, and the Betrayal of Reconstruction* (New York: Henry Holt, 2008), p. 137.

Chapter 14

"The attorney's recital . . ." *NOR*, February 26, 1874, p. 1.

"They kept me prisoner . . ." ibid., February 28, 1874, p. 5.

"A thrilling circumstance . . ." ibid., March 1, 1874, p. 1.
"They first came up . . ." *NOR*, March 1, 1874, p. 1.
"This statute is the law . . ." ibid., March 14, 1874, p. 1.

Chapter 15

"unconcerned with people . . ." Quoted in Anthony Champagne and Dennis Pope, "Joseph P. Bradley: An Aspect of a Judicial Personality," *Political Psychology*, Vol. 6, No. 3 (Sep., 1985), p. 485.
"My habits are these . . ." ibid.
"education was of the simplest sort . . ." ibid., p. 482.
"an engine of mischief . . ." Quoted in Lane, p. 192.
"the protection of these rights . . ." *New Orleans Bulletin*, May 22, 1874, p. 1.
"The Last Judicial Outrage . . ." ibid., June 11, 1874, p. 1, and June 12, 1874, p. 1.
"Judge Woods informed . . ." *NOR*, June 12, 1874, p. 1.
"The Fifteenth Amendment . . ." All quotes from Bradley's opinion found in *United States v. Cruikshank*, 25 F. Cas. 707 (C.C.D. La. 1874).
"that while he regarded . . ." *NOR*, June 28, 1874, p. 1.

Chapter 16

"His devotion to lofty aims . . ." *NYT*, May 8, 1873, p. 4.
"He was in important respects . . ." *BDE*, May 7, 1873, p. 4.
"about as well suited . . ." All quoted in Charles Warren, *The Supreme Court in United States History*, Vol. 3 (Boston: Little, Brown and Company, 1922), p. 346.
"fondness for controversy . . ." *BDE*, May 8, 1873, p. 2.
"When the Chief Justiceship . . ." Warren, p. 275.
"legal mediocrity . . ." *ibid.*
"knowing little of all law . . ." *BDE*, April 21, 1875, p. 2.
"President Grant has again . . ." *New York Herald*, December 8, 1873, p. 1.
"Judicial positions . . ." ibid.
"President Grant has a rare . . ." ibid.
"Evidently the President . . ." ibid.
"were not those given . . ." George H. Williams, "Reminiscences of the United States Supreme Court," *Yale Law Journal*, Vol. 8, No. 7 (Apr., 1899), p. 299.
"place political opportunity . . ." John S. Goff, "The Rejection of United States Supreme Court Appointments," *American Journal of Legal History*, Vol. 5, No. 4 (Oct., 1961), p. 365.
"packing his trunks . . ." *New York Herald*, January 10, 1874, p. 4.
"Morrison R. Waite . . ." Williams, p. 299.
"It is a wonder . . ." William H. Rehnquist, *Centennial Crisis: The Disputed Election of 1876* (New York: Alfred A. Knopf, 2004), p. 132.
"Mr. Waite stands . . ." Widely quoted. See, for example, Lane, p. 231.
"Although his practice . . ." *CDT*, January 20, 1875, p. 1.

Chapter 17

"equal rights in railroads . . ." *Congressional Globe*, 41st Cong., 2d sess., May 13, 1870, p. 3434.
"If the facilities . . ." Bertram Wyatt-Brown, "The Civil Rights Act of 1875," *Western Political Quarterly*, Vol. 18, No. 4 (Dec., 1965), p. 765.

"crown and complete . . ." ibid., p. 767.

"Champions of equal rights . . ." ibid., p. 770.

"whiling away the hours . . ." ibid., p. 772.

"All persons within . . ." Statutes at Large, 18 Stat. 335 (1875).

"It has put us back . . ." NYT, March 2, 1875, p. 6.

"At present, its effect . . ." CDT, March 1, 1875, p. 4.

Chapter 18

"The Democratic and White League . . ." "The White League Conspiracy against Free Government," a speech delivered by Hugh J. Campbell, 1875, privately printed pamphlet, https://archive.org/details/whiteleagueconsp00camp.

"McEnery and Penn . . ." On April 24, 2017, despite threats of violence, the monument was removed and placed in storage.

Chapter 19

"The first amendment . . ." United States v. Cruikshank, 92 U. S. 552 (1875); italics added

"eliminated from politics . . ." Warren, p. 327.

"To assume State powers . . ." Independent, April 13, 1876, quoted in Warren, p. 327.

"So far as the decisions . . ." NYT, March 29, 1876, p. 4.

Chapter 20

"to impress on the electorate . . ." Rehnquist, p. 85 (note).

"appealed to those . . ." John C. Nagle,. "How Not to Count Votes," Columbia Law Review, Vol. 104, No. 6 (Oct., 2004), p. 1734. The twentieth was for a disputed Republican elector in Oregon who was eventually allowed to cast his vote for Hayes.

"Republican Success Certain." NYT, November 6, 1876, p. 1.

"Reid spent election night . . ." Nagle, p. 1736.

"Results Still Uncertain . . ." NYT, November 8, 1876, p. 1.

"The Battle Won . . ." NYT, November 9, 1876, p. 1.

"Tilden was almost certainly . . ." Nagle, p. 1736.

"No one, perhaps not even Davis . . ." Roy Morris, Jr., Fraud of the Century: Rutherford B. Hayes, Samuel Tilden, and the Stolen Election of 1876 (New York: Simon and Schuster, 2003), p. 218.

"Bradley accepted the appointment . . ." Current-day Democrats have compared the election of 2000 with that of 1876. Chief Justice Rehnquist even wrote a book on the 1876 election in the wake of Bush v. Gore, in which he, not surprisingly, defended the role of the justices of both courts. Bush, however, at least involved an appeal in which the entire court could take a position. (That the resulting decision broke along party lines was not lost on its critics.) Bradley acted pretty much on his own.

"Reasonable men in both parties . . ." Allan Peskin, "Was There a Compromise of 1877?" Journal of American History, Vol. 60, No. 1 (June, 1973), p. 63.

Epilogue

"With the sounding of Taps . . ." Natchitoches Enterprise, July 6, 1922, p. 2.

ILLUSTRATION AND PHOTOGRAPH CREDITS

JACKET

Cover photos © Shutterstock: flag (pashabo), scratches (PrasongTakham), ornaments (vectorkat).

BOOK

Photos ©: cover flag and throughout: pashabo/Shutterstock; cover scratches and throughout: PrasongTakham/Shutterstock; cover ornaments and throughout: vectorkat/Shutterstock; 1, 2, 4, 5, 11, 15, 17, 19, 22, 29, 36-37, 38, 39, 41, 45: Library of Congress; 55: Architect of the Capitol/Flickr; 58, 61, 65: Library of Congress; 68: Historical/Getty Images; 71, 73, 74: Library of Congress; 76: Courtesy of HathiTrust; 81: Schomburg Center, NYPL/Art Resource, NY; 85: Library of Congress; 87: The Frent Collection/Getty Images; 88, 104, 106: Library of Congress; 108: The Granger Collection; 109, 117, 126: Library of Congress; 130: Fisk University, John Hope and Aurelia E. Franklin Library, Special Collections; 132-133, 148: Library of Congress; 152: The Johns Hopkins University Sheridan Libraries; 154: Library of Congress/Getty Images; 155, 164, 176, 181, 186: Library of Congress; 189: The Granger Collection; 194: Library of Congress; 195: 2017 Florida Center for Instructional Technology; 200-201, 203: Library of Congress; 205: The New York Historical Society/Getty Images; 207, 208, 209, 217, 218, 221: Library of Congress; 226: Billy Hathorn/Wikimedia; xix: Hulton Archive/Getty Images.

INDEX

Note: Page numbers in *italics* refer to illustrations.

Reconstruction Acts, 64–66, *65*
Reconstruction era
  and Compromise of 1877,
    221, 222
  conflicting perspectives on, 80–83
  end of, 222
  fallacies about, 123
  and Greeley, *108*
  Johnson's approach to,
    41–43, *41*
  and Joint Committee on
    Reconstruction, 59–60
  and Ku Klux Klan, 75–77
  Lincoln's plans for, 35, 41
  modern perspective on, 122–23
  perceived as a failure, 120–23
  and presidential election of
    1876, 216
  and Radical Republicans, 47–49,
    63–66, 120
  and rights protected by federal gov-
    ernment, 172
  Southern attitudes toward, 80,
    82–83
  Stevens's expectations for, 123
Redeemers
  Beckwith attacked by, 143–44
  Bruce's life threatened by, 129
  and elections of 1876, 129
  goals of, xvi
  massacre of freedmen in Colfax,
    xvii–xviii, xx
  memorial headstone erected in
    honor of, xx
  in political cartoons, *108*
  as portrayed by enemies of
    Reconstruction, 121
  and scalawags, 123
  and threat of federal prosecution,
    173, 175
  and voter intimidation, 129
  See also white supremacists
Rehnquist, William, 215
Reid, John C., 217

*Reminiscences of a Mississippian in Peace
  and War* (Montgomery), 82
Republicans and Republican Party
  and Bruce, 129
  and Civil Rights Act (1875), 196
  conservative, 97
  and elections of 1872,
    101–2, 113
  and elections of 1874, 191
  and elections of 1876, 215–22
  and Fifteenth Amendment, 102–3
  freedmen registering as, 66
  Liberal, 107–8
  and Philadelphia Centennial
    Exposition, 198
  power of, xvi
  shift away from Radical vision,
    166, 190
  split in, 107
  See also Radical Republicans
Revels, Hiram R., 124, *133*
Rhode Island, 12
Robinson, Harriet. *See* Scott, Harriet
  Robinson
Rutland, William, 115–16
Rutledge, John, 16

sailors, enslavement of foreign, 24
Sanford, John, 28
scalawags, 120, 123
schools, descgiegation of, 60
Scott, Dred, *29*
  birth and youth of, 24–25
  and *Dred Scott v. Sandford*, 27–28,
    30–32
  freedom gained by, 32
  marriage of, 27
  purchased by Emerson, 25
  relocation to New York, 28
  relocation to Wisconsin, 26
Scott, Eliza, 27, *29*, 30, 32
Scott, Harriet Robinson, *29*
  children of, 27
  freedom gained by, 32

Scott, Harriet Robinson (*continued*)
    and lawsuit for freedom,
        27–28
    marriage of, 27
    relocation to Wisconsin, 26
Scott, Lizzie, 27, *29*, 30, 32
secessionist states
    and Black Codes, 53
    divided into military districts, 64
    and Fourteenth Amendment, 63
    new constitutions of, 66–67
    post-war status of, 50–51
    and Reconstruction, 63–66
    and representation in House of
        Representatives, 51, 52–53, 63
    and voting restrictions on "rebels,"
        66, 83
    and white opposition to
        secession, 123
    white supremacist governments of,
        42, 48, 63, 67
    See also Confederates
Second Amendment of the US
    Constitution, 169
Second Battle of Liberty Place,
    207–9, *208*
segregation, 42
Seventeenth Amendment of the US
    Constitution, 3
Seymour, Horatio, 90, 101
Shelby, Alfred, 95, 96, 99
Sheridan, Philip, 66
Sherman, William Tecumseh, 72
slaves and slavery
    Bingham on, 58–59
    and Bradley, 168, 172
    and Bruce, 127
    and Constitution of United States,
        2–3, 31
    and Declaration of
        Independence, 197
    and *Dred Scott* decision, 28, 30
    and emancipation, 34, 46–47
    enslavement of foreign sailors, 24

and Jackson, 18–19, 20
Johnson's stance on, 40, 43
and marriage, 27
and Missouri Compromise,
    25–26
and number of representatives in
    Congress, 3, 6, 20–21
and political power of South, 21
runaways, 46
Rutledge's defense of, 16
and slave patrols, 70
and Southern culture, 20
and states' rights, 18–19
suing masters for freedom,
    27–28
Sumner's fight against, 188
and Taney, 22–23, 24
and Thirteenth Amendment,
    42, 47
and "Three-Fifths Compromise," 6,
    20–21, 51, 62
and Underground Railroad, 46, 142
See also black Americans
South
    and carpetbaggers, 66, *68*, 75, 81,
        120, 123
    dependence on slavery, 20
    and *Dred Scott* decision, 30–31
    and elections of 1868, 91, 101
    and Fifteenth Amendment, 103
    humiliation of, 83
    and Missouri Compromise, 26
    and number of representatives in
        Congress, 6, 51
    as portrayed by enemies of
        Reconstruction, 120–21
    post-Civil War economy of, 34
    and Reconstruction era, 35, 41,
        47–48, 80, 82–83
    and "Three-Fifths Compromise," 6,
        20–21, 51, 62
    violence in, 216
    Wilson on state of, 121–22
    See also secessionist states

ACKNOWLEDGMENTS

I'D LIKE TO ACKNOWLEDGE six very special people who were instrumental in bringing this book to fruition. Charlie Olsen at InkWell Management saw the potential in a changing market for a serious, hard-hitting book about a period in American history that has great parallels to our own, and then shepherded a most unusual proposal through what is often a byzantine submission process. Lisa Sandell at Scholastic, in addition to supplying sizable and quite gratifying doses of intelligence, enthusiasm, and commitment, demonstrated the trait most needed but not always found in an editor—genuine vision. Thanks also to Amla Sanghvi, photo researcher at Scholastic. Angela Onwuachi-Willig, who generally deals only with law students, saw the importance of bringing stories such as this to young readers and most generously agreed to write the foreword.

And, finally, my wife, Nancy, and daughter, Lee, who have the thankless job of putting up with me.

LAWRENCE GOLDSTONE has written more than a dozen books for adults, including three on constitutional law. This is his first book on that subject for young readers. Goldstone's writing has been featured in the *Boston Globe*, *Los Angeles Times*, and the *Wall Street Journal*, among other journals. He lives in Sagaponack, New York, with his wife, medieval and Renaissance historian Nancy Goldstone.